# HERBAL TEAS, TISANES AND LOTIONS

A guide to growing, preparing and using herbs for making stimulating tonics, soothing infusions and refreshing drinks.

*By the same author:*
FREE FOR ALL
HERBAL TEAS FOR HEALTH AND HEALING
HERBS AND FRUIT FOR SLIMMERS
HERBS AND FRUIT FOR VITAMINS
HERBS FOR ACIDITY AND GASTRIC ULCERS
HERBS FOR FIRST-AID AND MINOR AILMENTS
HERBS FOR HEALTHY HAIR
HERBS TO HELP YOU SLEEP

# HERBAL TEAS, TISANES AND LOTIONS

*by*

CERES

Line illustrations by Juliet Renny and Alison Ross
Colour photography by Paul Turner

THORSONS PUBLISHERS LIMITED
Wellingborough, Northamptonshire

First published 1981

British Library Cataloguing in Publication Data

Ceres
    Herbal teas, tisanes and lotions.
    1. Herbs
    I. Title
    641.3'57    TX406

    ISBN 0-7225-0677-5

Typeset by Harper Phototypesetters, Northampton.
Printed in Great Britain by
Lowe and Brydone Printers Limited, Thetford, Norfolk,
and bound by Weatherby Woolnough,
Wellingborough, Northamptonshire.

# CONTENTS

# INTRODUCTION

Purists among enthusiastic herb users insist that tisanes and herbal teas are completely different, so that the two descriptions should never be loosely used.

For the purpose of this book, the French word 'tisanes' is taken to mean the high proportion of drinkable infusions made from fresh or green herbs and from the same herbs that have been picked, bunched and hung up to dry. Slow-drying in a warm, dry but airy place means that the herbs lose their moisture but retain their vital properties and merely become crisp and storable. Nowadays, too, tisanes and lotions can be made from some green, frozen herbs that have been put in polythene bags and kept in a deep-freeze for future use.

For true herbal teas, plant leaves, young stems, branch-tips, flower-buds or even petals, have first to be subjected to different treatments. They have to be dried, possibly bruised, crushed or heated, or possibly also smoked, in order that the enzyme content of their tissues should be stimulated to cause the necessary change in their make-up. These processes bring about fermentation and produce quite a different and usually stronger flavour. The dried herb is then usually richer in tannin and some palates, especially those of smokers, find it preferable.

It is possible to bring about these necessary changes to the content of some herbal tissues at home by heating quantities of leaves etc., then bruising them and keeping them in an even heat, but it is far easier to be lazy and to buy commercially prepared Maté tea or, say, our familiar *Camellia sinensis* tea that have been all prepared and possibly blended with parts of other plants too.

Lotions made from single (or 'simple') herbs in the same way as tisanes (see page 29) and then used for *external* purposes — as complexion-improvers, hair-rinses and pain-relieving poultices, foments, compresses and dressings — have also been included. The benefits the herbs confer, when applied externally, are absorbed through the skin.

# PART ONE

# MAKING THE MOST OF HERBS

# CHAPTER ONE

# SOME BENEFITS OF HERBAL DRINKS AND LOTIONS

Although it is obviously delightful to be able to grow herbs at home for tisane and tea-making purposes and to provide beneficial lotions as well, it may not always be practical, in spite of all the advice given later in this book. It may be useful to know that, if these herbs have to be bought, the cheapest and most reliable way to obtain them is from well-known firms and there is a list of useful names and addresses of both growers and suppliers of herbal products towards the end of this book. In actual fact, not all the herbs mentioned here can be grown in our climate, so they have to be bought from firms that import them from reliable sources overseas, anyway.

If, however, it is feasible to grow only a very few traditional herbs at home, their value will quickly be appreciated. A few young leaves from a Borage plant, or a small handful of Chamomile flowering heads picked just before they are to be infused, make incomparably refreshing and delicious tisanes, which even after the gloomiest and most tiring day, quickly make everything seem sunny again. Home-grown herbs, like home-grown fruit and vegetables, when fresh and in season, have a superior flavour and are rich in vitamins. Even so, many of the herbs that are most commonly grown and are, perhaps, most easy to grow, do not stay green all through the winter and so must be stored.

Drying herbs for future use is very easy. The only thing to remember is that probably more of the herb is needed to bring the drink up to the same strength as when it has been made from fresh plants, and this seems to be the case when frozen herbs are used, as well. The conclusions obviously, too, can be drawn, that nothing tastes quite as good as when it has come straight from the earth's sources of invigorating and ever-renewing life-forces. Using stored herbs, though, is certainly better than doing without during non-growing periods.

## Some Medicinal Uses

For many centuries, a wide variety of herbs have been used to make drinks and to add to broths, soups and gravies, both for their flavour and for their remedial properties. Herb gardens were originally 'physic' gardens and it is gratifying to those of us interested in the benefits that using herbs can confer, that so many people are now returning, with appreciation, to using herbs carefully and with ever-increasing knowledge of their remarkable properties.

It is essential, though, to understand that self-medication for more serious, or even persistently recurring symptoms of a lesser degree, can be dangerous. It may be wasting valuable time if one does not go to a doctor or consult a qualified medical herbalist. The names and addresses of medical herbalists can usually be obtained from local health stores, or from the yellow pages of telephone directories, but you should make sure that they are fully trained and are members of the National Institute of Medical Herbalists, with the letters M.N.I.M.H. after their names.

### Indigestion

There are, even so, harmless herbs that can be used to ameliorate sudden little first-aid emergencies like those that bring such rapid relief for indigestion after too big or too rich a meal. Many carminative herbs, like Peppermint or Chamomile, have been used for generations to help 'to dispel the wind' and others are similarly useful if indigestible suppers cause restlessness at night.

### Bites, stings, rashes and burns

Many people have found their own innocuous herbal lotions for dabbing on insect bites or stings, or for sunburn and Nettle infusions are especially useful to help to quell 'the hot itch' of simple rashes and burns.

### Urinary troubles

Anyone who suffers from urinary troubles, ought to know the enormous help that can be gained by drinking tisanes and teas made from Blackberry leaves, Cornsilk—the long styles which form tassels at the tips of Maize cobs, (*Zea mays*), or of Parsley, and Parsley Piert leaves, when the urine smarts and burns (often because it is too acid). Some of these 'urinary herbs' act as mild diuretics and, by getting rid of some of the body's surplus water, they also act as 'slimmers'.

### Slimming herbs

Slimming endeavours can be greatly helped by trying either Cleavers or Fennel tisanes or *Maté* tea. The last makes such a satisfying drink that it can take away the need for fattening little carbohydrate snacks completely. Incidentally, an infusion made from the fresh leaves of Plantain (*Plantago major*) and taken in wineglassful doses, is said to be helpful to those who are anxious to give up smoking. It is also helpful, held hot in the mouth, for sufferers from toothache.

*Refreshing herbs*

As far as relieving natural fatigue after a day's work, tisanes may beneficially replace the felt need for alcoholic stimulants. Both Lime-flower and Elder-flower tisanes are very refreshing and lightly stimulating. Children in particular, enjoy them when sweetened with honey.

*Cuts, abrasions and wounds*

Herbal infusions used externally as lotions can work healing wonders on cuts, abrasions and wounds incurred from thorns in the garden. Marigold and St John's Wort are usually the first 'wound' herbs to be thought of, the former for clean wounds because of its fast-healing ability and the latter, if the skin injury has come in contact with soil. It is even said that St John's Wort, or *Hypericum perforatum*, acts as an antibiotic, but it is still important to consult a doctor to ask about the necessity for an anti-tetanus injection.

There are several splendid herbal infusions that can be used as foments to draw the inflammation out of festering sores or boils and surface abscesses. Marshmallow works apparent miracles at bringing these to a head so that no lancing is necessary to 'bring out the pus'.

*Complexion herbs*

Herbal lotions, apart from their many therapeutic uses, are very pleasing to make in normal strength or sometimes in concentrated form, for cosmetic purposes. Deliciously fragrant bathwaters and hair-rinses can be made from leafy branches of Lavender and Rosemary and the latter is said to be really beneficial for the hair. Complexion-improvers of many different kinds can also be made very cheaply at home from common herbs. They need not, actually, even be made from 'simples' (i.e. from one herb at a time) because different mixtures can be tried out with one herb being used to add fragrance. It should be remembered that, whatever the ingredients are, it is necessary to use them carefully and only in the usual proportion of ½-1 oz (15-25g) of fresh herb or one teaspoonful of dried herb to 1 pint (575ml) of boiling water, unless, that is, the solution is to be further diluted.

# CHAPTER TWO

# THE FASCINATION OF HERB GARDENS

There can be a fascination and a feeling of magic in old herb gardens where fragrant and aromatic shrubs and herbaceous plants are carefully cultivated and may have been growing for centuries. Many of them, too, are surrounded by a sense of peace, which emphasizes their simplicity and beauty.

Indeed, one of the most pleasant ways of learning to recognize the traditional herbs, getting acquainted with their appearances, as well as their habits of growth, is to wander round, or to sit and revel in an old herb garden. Some are still maintained in large gardens, usually where gardeners are employed, but on the whole it is the task of the mistress of the house to take care of her herbs. So, nowadays, because of the pressure of time, it is more practical to have neatly pathed and trimmed borders of these useful plants, than a lovely sprawl of Thyme or gracefully reclining bushes of Sage.

The small county *Gardens Open to the Public* booklets, where dated lists of opening times are usually accompanied by short descriptions of the gardens' contents, size and amenities, state where many herb gardens can be found. A little selection of some favourites is generally available, too, from bigger branches of public libraries. There is also a list of a few well-known herb gardens under *Herb Gardens,* towards the end of this book. Often, there are herb gardens included in such famous horticultural centres as The Royal Botanic Gardens at Kew, in Surrey, at Hampton Court, where there is a replanted knot garden, with the herb beds edged with low hedges, and at New Place, Stratford-on-Avon, with the addition here of Shakespearian redolence.

## The Romans: Early importers of herbs

There is a very interesting herb garden in the grounds of the Roman Palace, at Fishbourne, near Chichester in Sussex. The Romans were responsible for the introduction of a great many of our now familiar herbs. So, when some workers were building this magnificent palace, others were obviously given the task of creating a herb garden. The original plan was found when the excavations began only a few years ago, showing the layout of the buildings and gardens. Trenches full of imported soil, presumably for growing the imported herbs, were discovered, and those correspond exactly to the original layout patterns.

Since then, the modern gardeners have done all they can to try to find clues about the plants that the Romans themselves grew to enhance the flavours of Britain's native foods. As their knowledge has grown (much of it gleaned from Roman or subsequent literature) they have begun to replant the same herbs. This makes Fishbourne Palace particularly interesting because the garden adds so much to one's picture of the invaders' domestic life. Surplus plants, propagated by gardeners of our time, can be bought and taken home to provide memories of this ancient building and the importance of its place in the history of our island.

## Colour

Catalogues from specialist herb growers (see *Useful Addresses*) often describe variations of colour of foliage — golden, variegated, purple or even red-leaved strains — which can all be usefully employed to help us make our own beautiful herbal layouts.

Herb colours are enhanced, often at high summer, when the plants come into flower and lovely soft mauves, blues, pinks, yellows, creams and even reds can be enjoyed. Some of the herbal colours are not necessarily soft — think of the blue of Borage flowers (a favourite subject in many old embroideries), the striking royal purple of the Sages and the gloriously garish orange of Marigolds.

## Texture

The textures of herbs' leaves are equally important. They are often soft and hairy or, as a complete contrast, smooth, thick-skinned and shiny, perhaps rather small, thin and with in-rolled edges. There is more about the shapes and textures of these leaves later in this book, but they do add to the beauty and terrific diversity of patterns to be found in a herb garden.

## Scent

The scent that emanates either directly from these plants or after a leaf is picked, pressed and crushed, is possibly one of their most important features. It is linked, naturally, with the flavours they give, but each also stands alone as special and unique. Most herbs are at their best just before they come into flower and it is then, usually when the sunny days are long and hot enough to draw out the fragrance, that their essential oil content is at its highest. This is the best time for the sightless to visit the gardens specially designed for the blind, when there is the incidental pleasure too, of the sound of foraging bees and the songs of birds.

## Water Music

It is occasionally possible, even today, to have the additional pleasure of 'a little water music', which would certainly augment the pleasures given by a herb garden. No wonder British and European landowners and planners indulged their passions in the delicious sights and sounds of their towering fountains. Nowadays, in a new, small herb garden, we must be satisfied with, perhaps, a little ornamental pond; but, great ingenuity is needed to create some means by which moving-water sounds can be made. Water-garden specialists offer various 'cascade-making' suggestions, and even very simple fountains and spouts which may be turned on and artificially lit for special occasions. There is little doubt that most of us would, ideally, like a herb garden which included some water — even if it is a small pond, or even a bath for visiting birds! Remember, too, that visiting bees often get thirsty and need water in order to produce honey from the nectar, especially if it is over-concentrated when the weather is hot and dry.

## Sunshine and shade

Most herbs profit from being grown in sheltered areas, and they do not object to partial shade as long as they get sunshine for part of the day. This is a help to those of us, after coming down to earth from our dreams of idyllic herb gardens, who have shady gardens, or perhaps only patios or basement areas. In fact, it is quite possible to make a personal herb garden, in a tub, or a window-box or, sometimes, when necessity arises, indoors (see page 19).

If an actual herb garden, or very tiny growing area of herbs is not possible, it is delightful to read about others who have been able to bring their dreams to fruition and there are many lovely books (particularly those written nearer the start of the twentieth century by famous 'herb-women' such as Eleanour Sinclair-Rohde and Hilda Leyel), whose descriptions both of the gardens and of the herbs themselves, as well as of their histories, make enjoyable reading at all times.

# CHAPTER THREE

# GROWING AND STORING HERBS AT HOME

Growing decorative, aromatic as well as useful herbs at home can provide a most satisfying and successful hobby. Initially, it need not be expensive, as there are so many gardeners already who are ready to provide beginners with cuttings from their own plants, or possibly seeds, so that the only thing to think about is just where you will house your own collection.

**Indoor herb gardening**
Strangely enough, it is not essential to have an outdoor garden. Some herbs, like Mint, Parsley and Chives can actually be grown indoors. They need good light and plenty of thoughtful, loving care — otherwise, they make few demands.

Indoor herb-growing can be extremely therapeutic for invalids, or for those who are disabled and cannot get out as often as they might wish. The plants' very greenness, their beautiful shape and texture, the colours of their developing blossom and their actual growth pattern are all highly interesting to watch, to say nothing of the wonderful fragrance that they emit.

A small collection of herbs could be housed on the top shelf of a trolley. This could be moved about the room, for attention and for light just as the indoor gardener desired. Various herbs could be started off to make the little indoor 'patch' attractive and varied, and they might, perhaps, be enhanced, as they so often are in outdoor gardens, by colourful non-useful or inedible indoor plants such as a pot of Cyclamen, bulbs in a bowl, Indian Azaleas or an interesting *Schizanthus,* or Cape Primrose (*Streptocarpus* hybrid).

**Herbs in window-boxes**
There are plenty of useful herbs that can be grown in window-boxes and some, for example, English Marigolds, Borage and Thyme will produce colour as well as different growth patterns, so that this narrow 'bed' has a range of different heights, flowers and scents.

*Herb trolley*

Window-boxes, of course, are only specialized plant containers, made to fit certain spaces and the subject of growing herbs on balconies, patios, or in backyards, or even 'up the wall' with their roots in other types of containers, is very wide.

## Herb growing in containers

It may be as well, here, to discuss the containers even before planning out which plants are suitable to be grown in them. The important things to realize are that they need to have some provision for drainage and that they must be strong. Apart from their owner's aesthetic taste, it makes no difference at all what they look like. An old bucket or a tin bath, may look appalling while the plants in it are still very small but happy, full-time 'resi-dents' should grow quickly and soon hide the ugly contours. Such containers provide good, deep holders for the plants which, it is hoped, will survive for a long time.

It is important, too, to remember that a lot of our familiar herbs have been introduced from countries with warmer climates than ours, so that any growing here need as sunny a position as possible. They also need some shelter from cold winds.

Perhaps the example of old buckets and tin baths for containers was rather extreme. They were only mentioned to show that there is no need to spend a great deal of money on ornate and probably costly containers. Actually, all herb-growers can make do with a range of strong boxes that vary from shallow trays, for developing seeds and

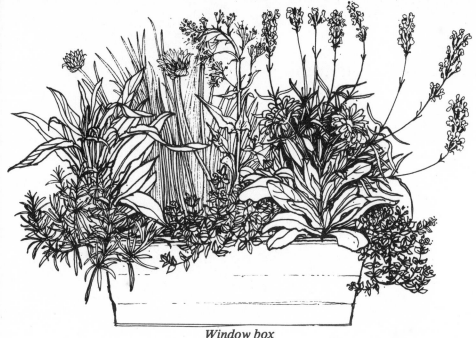

*Window box*

seedlings, to tubs made from wine-barrels, for plants with a longer life-span, such as small Bay trees.

There is one more point about container-growing that needs to be remembered. All container-grown plants need to have some waterproof tray underneath them. The exception being if they are standing on an outdoor surface that does not necessarily need protection.

### Watering

While on the subject of watering, it may sound ludicrous (but it happens to be true) that more plants, especially those in pots and other containers, are killed by over-watering than by under-watering. Anyone looking after plants of any kind needs to be able to learn to feel the soil sensitively with their finger-tips and so assess their plants' needs. It is interesting and surprising how quickly even beginners become aware of the water requirements of their plants.

Herbs usually need very little. Lavender, Rosemary, Marjoram and Winter Savory, even Sage, for example, all have leaves which are physiologically adapted to low rainfall in their sunny native Mediterranean haunts. The adaptations vary — some have hairy surfaces, some have very small, leathery skinned leaves with rolled edges — but these adaptations all mean that the surface from which their water-content may escape has some form of protection thus restricting evaporation. These measures help plants in sun-baked, or water-deprived situations to survive in periods of

*Container-grown herbs*

drought, so the occasional lapse on the part of their owners need not lead to fatalities.

Another important aspect about watering is that, as the water goes through the soil in the containers, it is likely to carry valuable soil nutrients with it. These may need replacing more often than they would in open gardens and so the application of fresh nutrients must be supplied in the form of organic composts and fertilizers.

## Propagation of herbs

Herbs can be grown from seed or, vegetatively, from cuttings. They can, occasionally, be grown by layering and, of course, they can usually be bought from specialist growers as already rooted young plants.

### From seed

It is probably better, despite offers from generous friends, to buy fresh seeds from seedsmen and specialist growers, if baby plants are to be started off in this way. It is essential to follow all the directions on the seed packets and do remember that seed germination can be a slow business. Annuals must be sown as seed.

### From cuttings

This process is undoubtedly faster in that you will have bigger plants more quickly and, in this case, offers of plant shoots from healthy parent-plants can be accepted graciously from friends. It is wise if you are a beginner-gardener, to watch every move that more experienced gardeners make and to ask any questions which will help you to understand what they are doing.

Some people insist that being 'green-fingered' and having great ability to get plants to 'take' and grow well, is an inbuilt gift. This may be so, but others fully believe that it can be acquired and that it is really basically available to anyone who is ready to learn the best way of making plants feel at home and to give them every chance to do well.

*Stem cuttings* can be taken at different times of the year: in spring, when most plants are starting to grow and are full of vigour; in mid-summer, just before or just after flowering; and in autumn, when they are subtly preparing to go into a period of dormancy to survive the coming cold weather.

Stem cuttings can be taken too, from side-shoots or the main shoots of perennials, shrubs and from trees, and are known, according to the age of the shoot and the state of its tissues, as

*Home-made propagator*

*Hardwood cutting (Sage)*

*hardwood, semi-ripe* or *softwood,* or *green cuttings.*

*Hardwood cuttings* should be pulled very gently away from their parent plant so that they have a 'heel' from its mature tissue still attached to them. Alternatively, they can be cut off straight with a sharp knife just below a bud. Both types should be about 8-10 ins (20-25cm) long. Their ends should then be dipped into hormone rooting powder before they are planted in a potful of potting compost. It is important to give all newly-growing plants a basically rich soil to start their growth in and the following commercially available composts can be useful at different stages of plant growth.

Those that are peat-based for seeds:

Levington Potting Compost.
J. Arthur Bowers General Potting Compost.
Rochford's House-plant Compost.

These must all be kept moist as they are difficult to soak again, once dry.

For those that are soil-based for plants beyond the seed-germination stage, use John Innes (or JI) types made up from silver sand, loam and fertilizer:

JI Seed Compost for seeds and cuttings.
JI No. 1 for potting-on seedlings and for rooted cuttings.
JI No. 2 for many potted plants, usually for large containers, as a top layer 10-16 ins (24-40cm) above good garden soil.

*Semi-ripe and green cuttings* taken in summer, should be taken from the current season's growth in exactly the

*Green cutting (Gillyflower)*

same manner, either with a heel of the parent plant tissue still attached to them, or by making a straight cut just below a bud. These can be somewhat shorter, possibly 4-8 ins (10-20cm), dipped into hormone rooting powder and planted and kept in a warm, humid place. A simple propagator to ensure good humidity in a dry place can be made by placing a polythene bag over light stick-props, see figure on page 23. This should be kept on until the cuttings have thrown out shoots.

*Root cuttings* from established herbaceous, thick-rooted perennials can often be successfully taken from the outside of the base of healthy, flourishing plants with a very sharp knife and then planted out and nurtured in the same way as those above.

*Root division* entails lifting the whole of the parent plant and dividing it up into smaller sections with a sharp knife. Only the strong and still growing parts of the older plants' roots and shoots should be selected for growing on. The old way of dividing perennial

*Root division of Liquorice*

plants by using two spades, thrust into the growing root, back to back and then levered apart, is now somewhat frowned upon.

*Layering* is another form of increas-

*Layering in ground (Thyme)*

ing plants by vegetative means of propagation. Layers can be started off with some herbs, like Thyme or from the low-growing procumbent shoots of Rosemary, Bay or Lavender. These shoots can be inserted into the top surface of the soil and weighted down, after being pegged and stripped of their leaves, and finally anchored by a dollop of moist, growing compost, covered by polythene.

*Air layering,* going through the same process as the above, could also be tried above the ground; selected shoots being surrounded by moist growing compost (or, in this case a good handful of damp sphagnum moss) and parcelled up into a polythene-covered 'sausage'.

## Compost for container plants

All growing plants need nourishment which they take from the soil, with moisture, through their roots in the form of soil nutrients. These are most easily available to them in rich loamy soils, with plenty of humus or dead leaf and other plant remains in it. As already said, the nutrients in container-

*Air layering (Bay)*

growing plants are rather freely and frequently washed through, so more have to be given in the form of natural composts and fertilizers. Some can be bought from nurseries and garden centres, but it is also worth making compost at home.

Compost for container plants is easy to make from all the raw vegetable and fruit waste from most people's kitchens. All these should be put into a big dark polythene bag which must be strong, on top of a layer of at least 2 ins (5cm) of garden soil which should be renewed between layers of this waste. Fallen leaves, collected from street trees can add to the compost's volume in small households, so can an occasional bag of seaweed collected from the seaside. This natural organic compost, after it has rotted down, provides a good source of soil nutrients and ought not to smell, even if it is kept indoors. The whole of the dark polythene bag's contents must be kept moist in order to encourage the rotting-down process and, if possible, should also be speeded up by putting it out on a balcony or verandah into the sun as it begins to fill up. Stronger, organic composts and fertilizers can be bought in concentrated form (the best are made from seaweeds), from nurseries and garden centres.

These instructions can, of course, be used for outdoor compost-making, putting the waste in a heap, straight onto the ground.

**Good companions**

It is extremely interesting that horti-culturists are beginning to find that some plants help others and that therefore, it is good to plant them near each other. Many of the culinary and aromatic herbs come into this 'good companion' category and it is thought they help to keep insect pests away by virtue of their fragrance and, sometimes, because of beneficial root-emanations.

The best known example of this is that of the onion family, which keep carrot-fly away if the carrots and onions are grown close together. Indeed, one of the strongest smelling of them all, garlic, is also said to be excellent for keeping roses free from green fly. Curiously enough, the magic works the other way round with roses, too, for they seem to promote a good, bright green growth of parsley if it is planted in the same bed.

What is so fascinating is that generations of country gardeners have put many of these natural partners together without understanding the reasons for doing so, often, one imagines, because they looked good together. Scientists are now finding out that old traditions were far more deeply full of wisdom than they would ever have believed.

Perhaps this was why the old herb beds in knot gardens in Elizabeth I's time were edged with such shrubs as box, or small forms of trees, such as yew. Both of these have a very strong smell and possibly provided natural protection as well as shelter for the plants that grew near. Several herbs, incidentally, including Parsley, Chives, upright forms of Thyme, and even low forms of Marjoram, can be used for edging vegetable, or even flower beds.

The old favourites, Nasturtiums, act as excellent companions if they are grown up the trunks of fruit trees, as they are said to help to keep them free from infections of woolly aphis, while Thyme, Peppermint and Hyssop are all believed to protect the Cabbage tribe from invasions of egg-laying white butterflies.

## Herbal plants that can be grown at home

The choice of plants that can be grown at home, as will be seen from the table towards the end of this book, is very wide indeed. It is, of course, wider, for those with gardens, but all the plants will need the same basic treatment and care, both during their initial growing time and for as long as they live. This will ensure that they give healthy leaves, shoots and sometimes roots or bark for using as tea-makers. Looking after herbs does involve careful observation and work, but the pleasure and benefits that can be derived are, for most people, ample repayment. There cannot be many who will not revel in the delight of picking tasty plants that they have grown themselves.

Some of the plants may need quite a lot of trimming and cutting-back or pruning to keep them at their best and in the correct size and shape. In this case, specialized books on the various subjects should be consulted, particularly if no expert is available to give first-hand advice.

In time, all growers come to the reluctant conclusion that their own collection of plants is getting too big. This is easily remedied, and it is a very rewarding time when one has enough plants to allow one to give away whole plants or cuttings to help others begin this rewarding hobby!

## Preserving fresh herbs for future use

### Drying

Herbs that are to be dried and kept for future use must always be gathered when they are at their best. This is usually just before they come into flower. Tradition says that they ought to be picked on a fine, summer morning as soon as the dew has dried.

They should be shaken gently, after being cut or picked, so that any small insects, spiders or other small creatures that may be sheltering in them are dislodged.

The herbs should be washed very gently, preferably under slowly running water, and then drained on a wire tray or, if small enough, in a colander. Any dead or disfigured leaves should be removed and the lower stalks left bare so that they can be tied into bunches to be hung, cut stalks uppermost, in a warm, dry, airy place out of the sun or any direct heat.

Different herbs take varying lengths of time to dry completely. Test them, from time to time, by breaking off a leaf or two to see if they are crisp and if so, give them a few more days so as to make sure that all the leaves are quite dry. Break the whole bunch up, rubbing the leaves and small young stems between finger and thumb, then pack the crumbled herbs lightly into screw-top jars. Keep these in dark, cool and dry places, but do not forget to label them carefully with the individual herbs' names.

Storing dried herbs in polythene bags is not recommended.

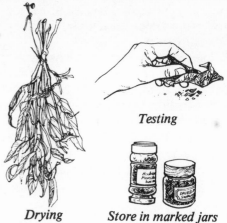

*Testing*

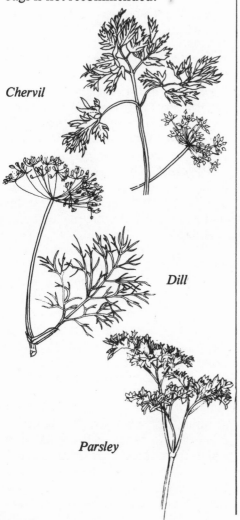

*Chervil*

*Dill*

*Parsley*

*Drying*     *Store in marked jars*

### Freezing

Some fresh green herbs, particularly if picked while still young, will last throughout the winter in a deep-freeze. It is a question of trying them out in small quantities, for yourself. Pick and prepare the herbs as for drying, drain them carefully and do not bunch them, but leave them loose before putting them into a polythene freezer bag. Remove as much air as possible and tie the bag up carefully.

*Rosemary ready for freezing*

# CHAPTER FOUR

# MAKING HERBAL TEAS, TISANES AND LOTIONS

First of all, get everything ready — herbs, lidded containers or pots or jugs, dry teaspoon and water, coming up to the boil. Then, if using a packet of dried herbs, or a sachet, read directions, carefully. If necessary, measure out the correct amount of herb and put it into a clean, dry container; then pour stated amount of boiling water onto it, put the lid on quickly and let it stand for the specified length of time to infuse, or 'brew'.

**Fresh herbs**
If using fresh, green herbs for tisanes, weigh out a ½-1 oz (15-25g) (or according to specific directions), wash carefully in fine strainer, then prepare and infuse exactly the same as with dried herbs.

Generally speaking, the most usual way of making tisanes, or herbal teas is to use one teaspoonful when they are dry, or ½-1 oz (15-25g) of fresh herb to 1 pint (575ml) of boiling water. However, this can be varied according to the taste of individual drinkers in the case of innocuous herbs like Mint, as can the length of time for infusing.

*Special herbal teapot made for the
author by a local potter*

## Decoctions

If the herbs are very hard or woody they
are likely to need decocting. This
means that they have to be boiled to
extract their essential ingredients. In
this case, put the required amount of
herb into a saucepan and cover as usual
with 1 pint (575ml) of boiling water,
then put on the lid and simmer gently
for the length of time suggested in the
directions.

Most tisanes and herbal teas are
pleasanter to take and to look at if they
are strained as they are poured into
their final drinking vessels.

*Other suitable pots*

## Dose

The recommended doses for therapeutic herbs vary from one teaspoonful, once, twice or three times a day, to
cupsful at varying times, perhaps
before any food first thing in the
morning, or before or even after meals.
The harmless and purely refreshing
herbs, taken for sheer delight, may be
taken when fancied, either hot or cold.
Iced Limeflower tea or a few others are
delicious, with the addition of
'floaters' (see below).

## Floaters

A few garnishing decorations, in the
form of safe flower, leaf or fruit
'floaters' can advantageously be added
to cool or iced herbal drinks to make
them look more attractive.

Ideas may be copied from the
'floaters' which are used more frequently for alcoholic drinks, like wine-
based 'fruit cups', or even the delicious
Pimm's No. 1.

Any of the following could be tried
as long as they are fresh: slices of
lemon, orange, red-skinned apples or
whole wild strawberries. Slithers of

cucumber or young radishes add flavour while Gillyflower or red Rose petals, Marigold florets and buds, blue Borage corollas, or whole Lavender flowerlets or Rosemary or Hyssop blooms too, would bring fragrance. Tiny sprigs of creamy Elder flowers, or Fennel or Caraway seeds, might also be a novelty.

A few of the flowers and their petals may be kept for future use if they are candied. This is a long process and involves boiling and re-boiling them in 1 pint (575ml) of water and 1 lb (450g) of castor sugar, every day for a week. No more water should be added, but additional sugar is a help. Temperature directions for candying (usually given for green Angelica stems) can be found in many cookery books which recommend the use of a sugar thermometer to expedite the process.

By the time most of the water has been boiled away, the then thickly-sugared parts of the flowers must be carefully lifted out and laid in rows on a rack which can finally be put into a just-warm oven to dry them off. They should be kept in air-tight glass jars with screw-tops, in places where they will not be disturbed (or shaken about as they are very brittle) until they are needed.

# PART TWO
# GUIDE TO HERBS FOR MAKING TEAS, TISANES AND LOTIONS

# CHAPTER FIVE

# INTRODUCTION TO LIST OF TEA-MAKING HERBS

It was difficult to decide how to compile this list of tisanes, tea-making and lotion-making herbs in this section. The scientific way would have been to arrange them under their Latin, scientific or botanical names because these are the same wherever they are used, be it Tooting or Tokyo. But the objection to doing this lies in the fact that, apart from botanists and horticulturists, very few people are truly conversant with them.

It is far more natural, when a few Dandelion leaves are needed for a salad or some young flowering heads for tea-making, to think of the plant as a Dandelion rather than *Taraxacum officinale!* So it seemed wisest to list all these herbs under their most common English names and then to put their Latin names, which are important to know, next, in brackets with a selection of local, popular, traditional names following. Dandelion (and other plants) have so many other names from all over Britain and Northern Europe, that it meant just choosing a few. Some

were almost too crude to include! These delightful country names, apart from being very picturesque, are also of great historical interest and can, at times, be guides as to some of the herbs' specific uses. Perhaps one of the best known examples of this sort of name is Eyebright (*Euphrasia officinalis*).

While on the subject of plants' country names, it is always worth enquiring of local inhabitants in different districts just what they call these plants. This can be, as I know myself, an absorbing hobby and can lead to a vast collection of alternative names.

But to go back again to the Latin names, these also frequently give interesting clues about the plants' properties. For example, the descriptive specific names of 'official', which has occurred in both the herbs that have been mentioned in this chapter means, medically speaking 'according to the Pharmacopoeia'. Nowadays, it is only an indication of the fact that plants so described were *once* included in the official Pharmacopoeia but not that they, necessarily, still are. As medicines have become more and more synthetic, obviously fewer and fewer plants have stayed in the British Pharmacopoeia, but some do still remain. Deadly Nightshade (*Atropa belladonna*) and Foxglove (*Digitalis purpurea*), both of which, unless used in minute doses and medicinally prescribed, are poisonous in the extreme (and are not included in this list!), are to the best of the author's knowledge, still in and so are Dill (*Anethum graveolens*), Coriander (*Coriandrum sativum*), Lavender (*Lavandula angustifolia*) and Mint (*Mentha arvensis*), to mention only a few of the best-known herbs.

There is another 'herbal' word which recurs, this time in the common English and in the country names and this is 'wort'; for example St John's Wort (*Hypericum perforatum*), meaning St John's herb, or plant. It comes from the Old English word 'wyrt'. Some etymologists, indeed, define the word 'wyrt' as describing a useful plant, so that this adds to its meaning when it is associated with herbs that are still in use today.

**Doctrine of Signatures**

Finally, in the following list you will find several references to the 'Doctrine of Signatures'. In the Middle Ages, when there was very little chance that anyone except the most erudite of monks who could consult archaic Herbals and certainly very few others could have read them, even if they had been available, some philosophers and those who loved and studied plants, devised this strange identifying guide. They tried to stress comparative similarity of plants' external appearance to parts of the human body or symptoms of illness of our bodies. Thus Lungwort (*Pulmonaria officinalis*), with its lung-shaped leaves, often with white spots on them, indicated that this was a good remedy for diseases of the lung. Greater Celandine (*Chelidonium majus*), its sap the crude yellow of raw bile, was suggested for liver-troubles, the liver being the 'manufactory of yellow bile'.

There are many of these indications. They are still interesting and many, like Eyebright (*Euphrasia officinalis*), with its spots within the eye of the flower, are still used by herbalists for the purposes designated to them by the old adherents to the theory. Although the Doctrine of Signatures has been mocked and scorned by scientists during this and the last century, there is possibly more ancient knowledge in it than modern plant-users have ever been able to establish.

# CHAPTER SIX

# ALPHABETICAL LIST OF TEA-MAKING PLANTS — NATIVE AND FOREIGN

**N.B.** An asterisk after the name of a herb in the following list indicates that it is possible to grow that particular herb at home, indoors, in a window-box or container or in the garden, so that tisanes can be made from its leaves. (See table on pages 116-121.)

**AGRIMONY** (*Agrimonia eupatoria*), Church-steeples, Tea-plant, Lemonade, Fur-burr, Catch-as-catch-can, Little Cocklebur. This wildflower is found in Britain and Europe. It grows in hedgerows, along woodland edges and on wasteland, with its yellow flowers towering up in a thin spire.

The whole herb is useful fresh or dried as a tea-maker. It can be drunk before meals, by the wineglassful, after having been infused in the usual way; a teaspoonful of dry, crumbled herb, which can be bought from a herbalist or health store, with 1 pint (575ml) of boiling water poured over it. It is good for those who need a tonic or a helpful blood-purifier. It is also now said to have antibiotic properties. Never, though, expect the action of herbs like Agrimony, to show dramatic results. There are only a few, mostly carminatives and external disinfectants and styptics, that show almost immediate effect.

**ALDER** (*Alnus glutinosa*), Whistlewood, Irish Mahogany, Aller and many other country names from various regions. This tree grows in Britain and Europe in damp marshy

*Agrimony*

*Alder*

places and produces beautiful deep-red, male catkins very early in the year.

Decoctions made from its shredded bark are useful as an external lotion for bathing swellings and helpful in making poultices (if used as hot as can be borne) for rheumatic joints. In the old days, bagsful of heated leaves were sometimes also used for this purpose.

*Alfalfa*

**ALFALFA\*** (*Medicago sativa*), Lucerne, Purple Medick. Usually called Lucerne in Britain, this plant is grown all over the world as a cultivated cattle-forage crop. It is a plant of enormous vitality, needing only one sowing to produce many crops of green growth. It can be found as a relic of cultivation, or as an escaper and can

also be planted in gardens. The seeds can be grown all through the year for salads and can be eaten whole as they first start sprouting. These do well indoors in jars where they can be kept moist, or in soil in pots.

Alfalfa makes an excellent tonic herb which also acts as a stimulant and a general 'pick-me-up'. It is useful for those who 'have become too lean' and a cupful of Alfalfa 'tea', taken three times daily, is easy to make from chopped-up young green growth which has been infused by having boiling water poured on it.

**ALECOST**
See COSTMARY.

**ANGELICA\*** (*Angelica archangelica*), Garden Angelica, The Angels' Herb. This tall fragrant herb grows wild throughout most of Europe but, in Britain it is merely naturalized and can occasionally be found along river-

*Angelica*

banks and canals. It is easy to grow in gardens, but needs plenty of space. Once sown it usually goes on sowing itself and seedlings come up all round the parent plant.

Angelica is used by herbalists as a digestive (carminative) herb, 'for those with wind in the stomach', also as a tonic and an expectorant and stimulative drink. It should be used fresh whenever possible. *It must not be taken by diabetics,* as it encourages the manufacture of too much sugar in the body.

The young stems of this plant and of Sweet Cicely (see page 103) both have synergic properties if cooked with very sour fruit, like gooseberries or rhubarb. They alleviate the acute sourness by working with the fruit juices to produce a sweeter taste. Possibly Elder flowers, which were often used by the older country people, always worked this same magic, too.

**ANISE** or **ANISEED\*** (*Pimpinella anisum*). This aromatic plant is cultivated primarily for its seeds. It can be grown in gardens in Britain but flourishes best in warmer mediterranean countries where the seed ripens freely.

Aniseed is used as a flavouring herb in many ways and a tisane made by pouring boiling water over a small amount of crushed seed or young leaves (the strength really is governed purely by taste) acts as a digestive and, in some cases, as an expectorant herbal infusion. It is said to be particularly helpful for hacking coughs and it is certainly loved (particularly when sweetened with a little honey) by babies. Aniseed tisane makes a very palatable and refreshing drink and it is delicious taken either hot or iced.

If Aniseed is planted in the garden, it should be carefully watched as the seeds begin to ripen because, once really ripe, the seeds fall and are lost.

*Apple*

**APPLE\*** (*Malus domestica cultivars*). Apple-water, or apple-tea can be made so easily and is a pleasing drink for those who are feverish. The apples should be washed, then sliced unpeeled and boiled gently until soft, then strained and sieved and a little brown sugar or honey added. This drink can be allowed to cool and then stored in a deep-freeze cube tray.

*Anise*

*Arnica*

**ARNICA** (*Arnica montana*), Mountain Tobacco, Accident-plant, Leopard's Bane. The flowers and roots of this plant are used to make a tincture which can be bought from some chemists and health shops and diluted by using a teaspoonful to 1 pint (575ml) of warm water. This dilution is strictly for *external use only*. It takes the pain out of sprains, bruises and unbroken chilblains, as well as muscular injuries if applied as a poultice. Arnica is a perennial plant growing on mountains in Europe (not in Britain) and other parts of the world.

Arnica is an old-fashioned remedy which still has many uses including that of making a refreshing foot bath for weary feet. The solution also has a reputation for making hair grow. *It should not be used if there are any open wounds, or scratches* where it is to be applied.

*Avens (wood)*

**AVENS** (*Geum urbanum*), Wood Avens, Herb Bennet, Goldy Star, Clove Root. This whole perennial herb is used as an infusion for curative purposes, especially for diarrhoea and dysentery. It is also recommended as a gargle as it has astringent and antiseptic properties. The root has a clove-like fragrance and used to be dried and powdered to put in moth-deterring bags among stored winter clothing. It was also used as a cordial 'against the plague', when the roots were boiled in water and, in the old days, earned the title of 'snake-bane' for its use in keeping off 'venomous beasts, including serpents'.

Avens is found wild in Britain in woods, hedgerows and even in untidy gardens. It has an unassuming yellow, starry, small flower followed by a head of hooked fruits and was once thought to be one of the holy herbs.

**BARLEY\*** (*Hordeum sp.*), Cultivated Barley, is often polished and is sold without an outer covering as Pearl Barley. Barley is now a frequently seen

*Barley*

*Basil*

crop which is harvested, bagged up and sold, among other things, as grain for cattle and for beer-making. Its straw is also sold as fodder and the grain has a multitude of purposes in the world markets.

However, the old way of boiling barley grains still makes a useful nourishing and diuretic drink if the soft grains are strained. Grain can also be added to stews, casseroles and broth to improve their nutritive content. Barley grains are soothing, particularly to the urinary system as they have a helpful demulcent quality. Barley water is better than plain boiled water for diluting milk if the latter is too rich for invalids or babies' food-drinks. Boiled barley makes a soothing poultice for abrasions.

**BASIL\*** (*Ocimum basilicum*), Sweet Basil. This familiar culinary flavouring herb is usually imported from mediterranean France and other frost-free regions. It is tender but can be grown indoors in Britain and Northern Europe. There are types with different flavouring properties; but the predominant one is clove/thyme-like. One sprig made into a tea or tisane, by having ½ pint (275ml) of boiling water poured over it and after being covered, left to infuse for a few minutes, makes a pleasant refreshing drink which can be made to look attractive by the addition of a slice or two of cucumber, orange or lemon, plus a few blue Borage flowers. It is thought to have mild antiseptic powers and, if sipped, to relieve nausea.

When a Basil leaf is laid on a dead Hindu's breast, it is believed that it acts as his passport to eternal paradise.

**BAY\*** (*Laurus nobilis*), Sweetleaf, Sweet Bay, Heroes' Crown. Bay is an evergreen shrub or small tree which is native to countries from around the Mediterranean. It grows well in parts of southern Britain, especially in coastal areas, although it also bears up well in towns and cities inland. It must be classed as tender as it dies in very prolonged periods of frosty weather but, generally speaking, it is a most useful plant for gardens, whether it is grown as a hedge or as single specimens. When there is room for it, Bay will grow up to nearly 6 ft (2m approx.) tall but on the other hand, short, severely trimmed Bay trees can be used as 'standards' in deep tubs, outside front doors.

*Bay*

Bay leaves, picked fresh, impart a fragrant, slightly spicy flavour to savoury rice, while it is being cooked, as well as to milk puddings, some soups and broths and to pasta dishes. The leaves need to be used with care as their flavour is strong and can be nauseating. This warning also applies when making a tisane: half a leaf to a quart (1 litre approx.) of boiling water makes a flavoursome-enough drink for most people. Taken like this, the resulting infusion is refreshing and carminative.

**BEARBERRY** (*Arctostaphylos uva-ursi*), Burren Myrtle, Dog-berry, Moanagus. Bearberry only grows in the Northern Hemisphere. It is a creep-ing evergreen shrub with leathery leaves and white or pink flowers. It is found on moors or mountains and forms dark mats of tough leaves. The leaves have a very old tradition of being useful for the treatment of bladder inflammations and are gathered and dried to be sold by herbalists and health stores.

*Bearberry*

Bearberry tea is made in the usual way — i.e. ½-1 oz (15-25g) to 1 pint (575ml) of boiling water — and is an antiseptic and very strongly astringent. If being kept for future use, it is important to keep the leaves completely dry. The tea is widely recommended for many urinary troubles and is said to improve the tone of the urinary passages as well as to alleviate the pain and discomfort of the inflamed bladder and urethra for cystitis patients.

**BEE BALM** or **SCENTED BALM.** See LEMON BALM.

**BERGAMOT, RED\*** (*Monarda didyma*), Bee Balm, Oswego Tea, Scarlet Mop. This garden plant, which

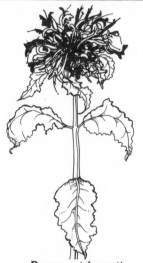

*Bergamot (sweet)*

is native to North America, grows well here in flowering herbaceous borders and is a great attraction to bees. The whole growth is fragrant and a few of the young leaves when picked fresh, can be used as they are and have been for a long time in America, for making a delightfully scented and refreshing herbal tea. This is helpful for headaches and nausea.

Bergamot plants can be propagated by root division and by deep cuttings. The heads of flowers, which can also be pink, provide a brilliant patch of colour in the summer garden.

**BETONY** (*Betonica officinalis*), Bishop's Wort, Bitny, Sentinel of the Woods. This wildflower with a tight, terminal head of dark crimson flowers, used to be said to be abhorrent to children. Even so, it had the reputation of being a holy herb with powers for holding off witches, devils and other evil spirits.

An old Herbal compiled late in the seventeenth century says 'Tis hot and dry, acrid and bitter . . . it opens and cleanses.' Another recommended it as 'a very precious herb'.

As a herbal medicine now, Wood Betony is picked when it is coming into flower and then dried in a warm place, to be used as an astringent nervine. It is 'Useful for hysteria, but also for a tonic and alterative. A few leaves infused in boiling water still proves to be a helpful drink for those who feel completely languid and have slight nervous headaches and for those who loathe and cannot digest their food.'

*Betony (wood)*

**BILBERRY** (*Vaccinium myrtillus*), Whortleberry, Hurtleberry, Hurts, Blackhearts. This wild plant has so many popular country names that it is impossible to quote them all. Such a vast number, though, does denote a plant's usefulness and good reputation and Bilberries are sought, when ripe, on moors and mountain-sides in many parts of Britain and Europe.

*Bilberry*

The berries are not only used as fresh fruit and for cooking but some are now frozen as well as being dried, for future and winter use. A few soaked in boiling water make an acid tea which has an old traditional acceptance of being useful to diabetics. It is also useful as a quick cure for diarrhoea, especially when the fruit is also eaten. Herbalists use it for a variety of bowel complaints. The tea makes an excellent astringent gargle with healing qualities and provides a body that has been deprived of vitamins with an internal anti-scorbutic remedy.

The leaves, picked and dried, are also helpful in the same way as those of Bearberry (see page 42) for making a drink to help those with urinary troubles.

*Birch (silver)*

**BIRCH, SILVER\*** (*Betula pendula*). Everyone knows this graceful tree with its bark that pulls off in strips, leaving a pale new under-surface. It may not be known, however, that the young fresh leaves, made into a tisane and sweetened with a little honey, are an excellent after-winter tonic which is also said to be good for gout and rheumatic complaints.

**BISTORT\*** (*Polygonum bistortum*), Easter Giant, Passion Dock, Poor man's Cabbage, Snakeweed, Patience Dock, is another wild British and European flower with a host of country names. It is a member of the same family as Sorrel, though its leaves appear earlier than the two more common Sorrels. These leaves have long been used as a green vegetable and for making teas and health-beers, usually near Easter-time, just as the effect of the long, cold winter, with its shortage of fresh vegetables and fruit, is beginning to be felt.

Bistort grows sparingly in damp meadows, or in 'old meadowland'

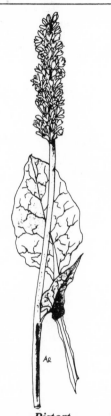

*Bistort*

*Blackberry*

which has not been destroyed and re-sown with weedless grass-seed mix-tures. It can, however, be grown in gardens from seed bought from herbal nurserymen and is a useful herb to have both for eating raw in salads and for tea-making. It is a strong astringent (its juice can be used as a styptic), and it helps all bowel complaints, piles and nose-bleeding.

**BLACKBERRY\*** (*Rubus fructico-sus*), Bramble, Blegs, Scald-head, Bumble-kite. Ripe blackberries make a delicious tea if boiled just long enough

to make their pulp soft and sievable. The juice should then be poured over some pale, soft brown sugar. Their leaves, too, have medicinal properties, being highly astringent and also good to take, in tea-form, as a urinary tonic or alterative. A lotion made from blackberry leaves can be used extern-ally for cosmetic purposes and is said to be good for 'acne, the black and the white-heads'. It can be used as a gargle and mouthwash, too.

Cultivated, thornless varieties of Blackberries can easily be grown in gardens.

**BLACKCURRANT\*** (*Ribes nigrum*). A delicious drink can be made from fresh or dried or frozen blackcurrants, in the same way as one from Black-berries. If fresh fruit is used, the resulting tea can be sweetened and then frozen and for those that grow this soft fruit, it proves to be far cheaper than

*Blackcurrant*

buying Blackcurrant cordials by the bottle. If you have made it yourself you also know exactly what it contains.

All aluminium pans should be avoided in fruit-cooking, as their use can sometimes upset people.

If any Blackcurrant drinks or home-made syrups prove to be too sweet, the addition of a little fresh lemon juice improves them and adds to their vitamin content.

**BLACKDERWRACK (***Fucus vesiculosus***)**, Kelp, Sea-wrack, Popper Seaweed. This brown seaweed is common around all parts of our shores and other north Atlantic coasts. Its fronds grow long and have inflated bladders, usually in pairs, which help to keep the plant in a floating position away from the sea-bottom and rocks from which it grows.

Bladderwrack should be *picked* (not gathered in a cast-up, possibly stale, state off beaches) from rocks which are only exposed at low tide. It should then be dried in warm, but not sunny, places.

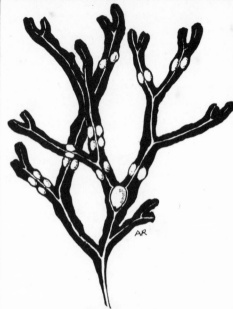

*Bladderwrack*

Infusions made from it should be taken very sparingly in wineglassful doses, three times daily, for a few days only at a time. It is a useful diuretic and incidental 'slimmer'.

A 'boil-up' of this seaweed makes a soothing (even if somewhat slimy) poultice, or compress for rheumatic wrists and knees.

**BLUE FLAG\* (***Iris versicolor***)**, American Swamp Iris. A beautiful slender iris which can be grown in gardens in Britain and Europe, but which needs marshy soil. Lotions can be bought that have been made from the dried root of both this and the commoner German Iris or Flag, which are wonderful complexion-clearers and softening to the hands. Most of the irises have emollient properties.

*Blue Flag*

Tea made from the dried and ground root of the *Iris versicolor,* and taken internally, acts as a tonic and a blood-purifier.

**BORAGE\*** (*Borago officinalis*), Bee's Home, Bee's Rest, Burrage. Once sown in a garden, this beautiful herb with cobalt-blue flowers usually regenerates itself. It is an annual and an asset to any herb garden, as well as to rough corners or untidy borders. The inch-wide flowers have black centres and used to be used as far back as the Middle Ages as models for embroidery. They can also be picked and crystallized (they do not freeze well,

unfortunately) and used to decorate salads and to float on top of lemonade and other drinks.

*Borage*

All parts of this plant are harmless, so that the young leaves, too, can be picked and dried or chopped up and used to make 'green tea' for a tonic and a cheering cordial. Biochemists have now discovered that the plant lives up to its old reputation of 'I, Borage, bring courage' because it acts as a stimulant to the adrenal glands. So try Borage tea (made from the fresh leaves) for low spirits and times when you need a boost. It also has an old reputation for being useful to sufferers from rheumatism.

**BUCHU** (*Agathosma betulina*). A small shrub growing in South Africa, the leaves of which are mostly gathered round the Cape and dried and exported to the U.S.A. and Britain for their medicinal virtues. They can be bought from health stores and herbalists and are excellent as a tea-making herb for those who suffer from cystitis and other urinary troubles. Buchu is also said to make a useful tonic-tea but it is chiefly used — indeed almost as a

*Buchu*

specific — as a tea herb for catarrh, inflammation and soreness of the bladder.

**BURDOCK** (*Arctium lappa*), Cocklebur-plant, Sweethearts, Happy Major, Beggar's Buttons. This familiar British wild flower is often named Burr-top too, because of its heads of hooked fruits which attach themselves to passers-by's clothing and to the fur and wool of animals, so ensuring their wide

*Burdock*

dispersal away from the parent plant. (See also Agrimony on page 37.)

The huge leaves are traditionally associated with butter-making as they were used by dairymaids to wrap butter in. They are said to be slightly cooling or even refrigerant.

While still young, the leaf-stems can be boiled as a free, wild vegetable and the whole leaves can be picked, dried and used for a tisane-making herb which is a first-rate tonic and blood-cleanser. Externally, the tea or lotion can be used as a poultice for stubborn sores and unhealing ulcers.

Ripe seeds can also be collected and when their rough outer coatings are discarded, they can be eaten like sunflower seeds although they are very much smaller. They are sometimes infused to make a gentle diuretic.

**BUTCHER'S BROOM\*** (*Ruscus aculeatus*), Shepherd's Myrtle, Knee-holly. No-one would believe that this spiny, dark and stiff evergreen shrub could belong to the Lily family (*Liliacae*), because its flowers are most insignificant and of a pale greenish white in colour; they measure only about 10mm in width and grow out of the centres of the spiny-tipped flattened stems, or cladodes.

The root (which, if dug up, means the destruction of this plant), can be easily grown in most gardens, and used to make an infusion that is believed to be extremely good as a herbal drink for those who suffer from jaundice, dropsy or gout. It can be sweetened by the addition of a little honey and

*Butcher's Broom*

drunk, in a wineglassful dose, first thing in the morning 'to relieve the fighting for the breath and to loosen the phlegm on the chest'.

The very young, soft green shoots can be picked for cooking, like Asparagus, which is another member of the Lily family.

There is, however, a warning about using this plant, as it is thought to be unsuitable for sufferers from high blood pressure.

**CALAMINT\*** (*Calamintha sylvatica*), False Catwort, Bruisewort. This is a small but spicily fragrant herb which grows wild on chalky banks and in downland hedgerows. It can easily be cultivated in gardens and makes a change from the flavours of ordinary Mints and Thymes.

The dried leaves are sometimes prescribed by medical herbalists for use as a sweat-stimulator during feverish colds and also as an expectorant for the tenacious mucus which follows winter ailments, as well as a tonic herb. Apart from this, Calamint makes a pleasant cordial infusion and one which Culpeper said 'is good for the brain'.

The scalded leaves can be used as a poultice to 'lift' persistent bruises.

*Calamint*

**CAMELLIA** (*Camellia sinensis*), Tea. Perhaps it is not generally known that all our everyday tea is made from the dried leaves of special Camellia shrubs which are cultivated in the East. Both black and green teas are made from the

*Camellia*

same plant, the differences in the finished product beginning in the drying and fermenting processes.

As it is known today, Tea is a stimulant and astringent drink with definite nervine properties. It contains the substances theine (allied to caffeine) and tannin and the regular practice of drinking strong tea is definitely harmful to the human system.

**CARAWAY*** (*Carum carvi*), Caraway seeds (whole or ground up) provide excellent flavouring for cakes, vegetables and savouries. They can usually be bought at delicatessens and health shops but are less easy to obtain than they used to be. It is possible, though rather chancy, unless there is a good, hot summer, to grow the plant in a sheltered and warm garden in Britain but frequently the seeds, which are the most important part, do not ripen and so cannot be harvested.

A delicious tea can be made from the whole of the herb if used when very young. It is refreshing and acts as a mild

carminative but it is the crushed seeds, which when infused — a teaspoonful or less to 1 pint (575ml) of boiling water — provides the real carminative. Some people find they are more helpful, when they are boiled. Those who find cooked cabbage particularly indigestible benefit from the addition of a few caraway seeds when cooking it. Certainly they impart a pleasing flavour to cooked white cabbage.

Herbals generally regard Caraway to be one of the best stomachics, and it is also completely harmless.

*Carrot*

**CARROT*** (*Daucus carota*). Wild carrots, from which our red and fleshy root vegetable has been developed, are sometimes known by the pleasing country name of 'Bird's-nest'. This name must have arisen from the way the withered flower-umbel 'is drawne together when the seede is ripe, resembling a birde's nest', as an old herbalist describes it.

*Caraway*

Carrot tea can be made by boiling young carrots gently, without salt, and allowing the water to cool before being sipped, when it is thought to be good for digestive troubles. It is not particularly recommended, however, as from personal experience the author has found that raw, 'juiced' carrots provide a far more acceptable and healthy short drink.

*Catmint*

**CATMINT\*** (*Nepeta cataria*), Catnep, Cat's Delight and Catwort. This plant might also be christened 'Butterflies' Delight' as it attracts a multitude of butterflies, particularly Peacocks and Small Tortoise-shells. It is easy to grow in gardens, from seed or by root division, but an old saying tells of its attractions for cats, which like to roll on it:

If you set it, the cats will eat it,
If you sow it, the cats don't know it.

This possibly refers to the fact that the scent is stronger while the plant's leaves are immature.

A tisane made from the flowering tops has carminative virtues (like so many of those made from other members of the Labiate family) and it has also been thought to make a good tonic and to be mildly stimulating.

**CELANDINE, GREATER** (*Chelidonium majus*), Swallow-wort, Devil's-milk, Wartweed, Witches'-weed. The use of the final old popular name showed that this plant was to be treated with respect and this reputation still holds good. *Never use Greater Celandine unless it is prescribed by a medical herbalist.*

This is now a fairly uncommon wild plant, growing near old habitations, often on rough walls, or in the shelter they provide. It is totally different in appearance from the Lesser Celandine as well as being botanically unrelated. It was frequently used by country people to help in the cure of bad bilious attacks and jaundice because the whole plant exudes a bright yellow (bile-like) juice. (See page 36 for an explanation of the Doctrine of Signatures.)

An infusion made from the whole herb, collected and dried when it is at its best in early summer, is sometimes prescribed as an alterative and to help stubborn eczema and other difficult skin complaints. If the raw, undiluted juice is used externally as a wart-cure, great care must be taken to see that it does not get onto any surrounding skin surface as it is a strong corrosive.

**CELANDINE, LESSER** (*Ranunculus ficaria*), Pilewort. 'Wort' is an ex-

*Celandine (lesser)*

tremely ancient word meaning a herb or useful plant and this plant is very common as an invasive garden weed and as an attractive, early-flowering wildflower.

As a lotion-providing herb *it should never be used internally,* but when used externally as an infusion or lotion — made by pouring boiling water over ½ oz (15g) of the whole herb — it is occasionally recommended to soothe haemorrhoids or piles *as long as they are not bleeding or open.* Hence, presumably, its country name.

The roots of Lesser Celandine are tuberous and resemble the unpleasant physical appearance of bad, pendulous piles, so the name may only have come from this superficial similarity.

**CELERY\*** (*Apium graveolens*). Water in which Celery has been boiled should always be saved and drunk as a herbal tea. In fact any of the raw, or cooked parts of the plant are most valuable, especially for anyone with any rheumatic problems. Even Celery salt, which can be bought at delicatessens and health shops, is useful and greatly improves salads and other vegetables and savouries.

*Celery*

Curiously enough, Celery tea is also a mild sedative and some people drink it before going to bed. It is a 'slimmer', too, being a diuretic herb which is completely harmless, but should not be taken in excess.

*Centaury (pink)*

**CENTAURY** (*Centaurium erythraea*), Earth-gall, Feverwort. This delightful, small wildflower has been used by herbalists throughout the years for a wide variety of purposes. Its second country name tells of its propensity to act as a febrifuge and it is also said to be a bitter tonic and a blood-purifier. It is sometimes prescribed by modern herbalists to be taken with Agrimony (see page 37) when it acts to reduce the temperatures in malarial fever or in complaints with similar symptoms.

The bought herb is collected and dried and can be infused in the usual way. Applied externally to the skin it has the old reputation of discouraging fleas and lice!

Culpeper says that 'the herbe is so safe that you cannot fail in the using of it. . . . 'Tis very wholesome, but not very toothsome.'

*Chamomile I*

**CHAMOMILE I\*** (*Chamaemelum nobile*). Common Chamomile, Maythen, English or Spanish Chamomile. This herb, which does grow wild but is difficult to identify, can be grown with great ease in most gardens. Seeds can be obtained from herb-growing nurseries and once sown, if a few flowers are left to go to seed every year, it will prove to be self-regenerative. The flowers are the part to dry for future use for teas.

It is certainly one of our most popular and useful herbs and almost, to some people, a panacea for all minor ills! Chamomile tea is helpful for sleepless, and teething or otherwise fretful babies (when it should be sweetened with a little honey), as well as for sleepless and frustrated adults. It is also excellent for indigestion and for hysterical and less fearsome nervous symptoms.

Externally, Chamomile lotion is splendid as a complexion-wash as well as for 'giving new life to tired blonde hair'. Strong Chamomile infusions added to bath-water, 'ease the tiredest body and the spirits too'.

For internal purposes Chamomile tea needs, like most other herbal drinks, to be brewed in a lidded pot, jug, or beaker.

**CHAMOMILE II** (*Matricaria recutita*), German Chamomile. This second Chamomile can again be found growing wild, usually in waste places or arable fields but again, because of difficulty of identification, it is wiser to grow it from accredited seeds, which should be sown in autumn. The plants will come into flower the following summer. The plants will re-seed themselves if some flowering heads are left to ripen and scatter.

*Chamomile II*

The fresh or dried flowers are an even stronger carminative tea-maker than Chamomile I. They make harmless drinks for all the same purposes, including that of soothing fretful babies and irritable, often flatulent adults, too. Doses should be varied according to age and a couple of small teaspoonfuls should be enough for the very young. Adults can sip at a wine-glassful of this herb's tea while it is still fresh and warm and, perhaps, sweetened with a little honey.

**CHERVIL** (*Anthriscus cerefolium*). The whole of this plant can be cut and used to make a green tisane, in the usual 1 oz (25g) to 1 pint (575ml) of boiling water proportions. The resulting infusion also makes an excellent poultice-soaker for painful wrists, ankles and knees.

Chervil is, of course, a good plant for eating raw, especially when young, and makes a tasty addition to salads.

*Chervil*

**CHICKWEED** (*Stellaria media*), Chicken's Meat, White Birdseye, Mischievous Jack. I have never actually found that 'little birdes in cages' are particularly delighted if a tuft of this plant is pushed through the bars for them to peck at, but there is no doubt that it is full of vitamins. I have, though, seen wild goldfinches and linnets descend on it in packs, once it is in seed in fields.

It is an invasive weed but it can be useful to keep some in gardens. If it is hoed off, *before it seeds,* Chickweed makes good green manure if used in compost, or it can even be turned in to the soil. When picked, while still young and tender, it can be used for salads or can even be cooked as an extra early spring vegetable.

A small handful of rootless Chickweed can be infused to make a good complexion-wash or lotion for winter-weary skins as it is demulcent. It is particularly useful for chapped hands and a poultice made from hot Chickweed lotion makes a useful foment for boils and carbuncles.

*Chickweed*

*Cinnamon*

Taken internally Chickweed tisane, made in the usual way, is thought to be a 'slimmer' if three wineglassesful a day are taken before meals.

## CINNAMON (*Cinnamomum zeylanicum*).

This spice is grown and collected so that it can be prepared in dry or essence form from the inner bark of a tree grown in Sri Lanka (Ceylon) and the East Indies.

The essence is fragrant, familiar and known as an internal disinfectant which is useful for preventing colds and for helping to alleviate their effects even after they have been caught. It is a popular remedy and can be bought from chemists and taken according to directions on the bottle. Powdered cinnamon can be bought in health shops and delicatessens for culinary purposes.

Cinnamon makes a spicy drink which is said to cleanse the mouth, throat and 'pulmonary tubes'. It also has a carminative, stimulant and pleasant flavouring effect. Some people find that it makes a good cure for nausea if sipped, when warm, very slowly.

## CLEAVERS* (*Galium aparine*),

Goosegrass, Little Sweethearts, Hayriffe, Robin-run-in-the-hedge, Mutton-chops, Everlasting Friendship. This wild plant, common in Britain, Europe and in parts of the U.S.A., is well known as can be seen from its huge number of local and popular country names. It is also a useful and quite pleasantly-flavoured tea-making herb.

The tisane can be drunk by 'they who are sleepless', it acts as a diuretic for those who wish to slim and is most helpful for people with urinary troubles. Externally, it makes a good skin-wash for 'removing ugly freckles' and is helpful as a lotion for sore sunburn, insect bites and stings.

The whole young plant can be gathered and used as a green vegetable, providing it is not picked after the stems have become fibrous. Chopped-up, raw Cleaver stems and leaves can be added to green salads.

*Cleavers*

The small round pairs of hooked fruits (hence the names of 'Little Sweethearts' and 'Everlasting Friendship') can be gathered from wild plants and sown in an uncultivated corner in the garden. Children from time immemorial, have pulled Cleavers stems out of hedges and stuck them on the backs of companions and passers-by. They stick on because of the general hooked-hair covering of the leaves and stems as well as of the fruits, but may not always ensure 'everlasting friendship' as they are sometimes difficult to get off! The mechanism of the hooked fruits (which frequently get into animals' coats and are horribly awkward to remove) is, of course, a means of seed . dispersal (see also Agrimony and Burdock).

**COMFREY\*** (*Symphytum officinale*), Gooseberry-pie, Suckers and Sweet Suckers, Church Bells, Pigweed. Comfrey grows wild in damp meadows and on waste ground; it can also be cultivated, advantageously, in gardens. It is a most useful herb, both for infusions and to eat raw, chopped when the leaves are young, for salads and sandwich fillings or even to be cooked as a vegetable.

It has a great reputation for mending bones, in fact two of the less common popular names are those of 'Boneset' and 'Knitbone' as the leaves used to be used wet and applied to the skin over simple fractures. They are slightly mucilaginous and so 'set' as more and more were layered on, into a kind of vegetable plaster.

Comfrey is an ingredient used in many ways by herbalists in many different British, American and European countries. The plant contains the important substance allantoin, which is known to act as a vitalizing healer. The whole plant is dried for winter use

*Comfrey*

and very young and tender Comfrey leaves, when picked immediately before the bagging-up process starts, can sometimes be successfully frozen in a deep-freeze. They can also fail to stay green, so try freezing only a few at a time at first.

Tea made from fresh and dried material or from a few drops of tincture (obtained from health shops or herbal chemists) can be taken for ulcers of the stomach, all kinds of inflammation of the lungs, coughs and for the allev-iation of the pain from internal hae-morrhoids (piles). It is also good to soothe the bowels and often acts like magic in cases of diarrhoea.

Externally, apart from uses already mentioned, it can be used as a lotion for all wounds or minor burns and scalds and sunburn.

*Coriander*

**CORIANDER\*** (*Coriandrum sativum*). This herb, native to mediterranean areas, has a distinctive taste that is eagerly sought in the East and West. It used to be cultivated in East Anglia and relics of cultivation and odd speci-mens, from foreign seed, do still turn up among other crops.

It is a small umbelliferous plant which can be grown in gardens that are warm and sunny, but the important part is the seed which needs to be ripe in order to be dried for future use. If it is grown and is freely available, young leaves can also be used sparingly in salads. The fresh seeds smell like old cloth but their flavour is orange-like and unique and strong. They are one of the ingredients of curry and they have many virtues ascribed to them. The Chinese thought they conferred ever-lasting life on their eaters!

Nowadays Coriander seeds are beginning to come into their own because they are good for rheumatics and arthritis, and a small teaspoonful of seeds infused in 1 pint (575ml) of boiling water and drunk three times a day by the cupful, acts as a carminative and an antacid.

**CORNSILK\*** (*Zea mays*), Corn-on-the-cob, Maize. The large strong growth of maize is grown as a fodder crop for animals, as well as for a garden vegetable for humans. Towards the autumn, heads of intricately arranged 'seeds' form and ripen and each is topped by a long, dark red style. These form a tassel at the top of the cob and are extremely useful when made into a herbal tea for sufferers from urinary complaints, especially from sudden cystitis. The tassels are actually called, in popular language, 'cornsilk'.

Cornsilk tea is demulcent and very soothing to sore urinary passages and it also acts as a diuretic. It is made, as my herbalist once said, by putting a large pinch (i.e. as much as can easily be picked up between one's thumb and first finger-tip) of the dried herb into a beaker and filling it up, but the rule that is generally accepted is that 1 oz (25g) of this herb is infused in 1 pint (575ml) of boiling water which can be sipped, when cool enough, at intervals all through the day. Its effect, as long as a good swig or even a mugful, is taken initially, is surprisingly quick.

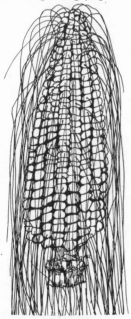

*Cornsilk*

**COSTMARY\*** (*Chrysanthemum balsamita*), Herbe Sainte-Marie, Alecost. This is a well-known garden herb with a particularly spicy flavour which is useful for culinary purposes. It is simple to grow in any soil, from cuttings and root division. It is said to

*Costmary*

increase the fragrance of neighbouring herbs.

Apart from its uses for flavouring herbal beers (hence the old name of 'Alecost') it is seldom used for infusions, but some herbalists still prescribe it as a stomachic.

**COUCH GRASS** (*Agropyron repens*), Twitch, Dog-grass. This creeping grass is one of the gardener's worst weeds as, once it has a hold in a garden, it is almost impossible to get rid of.

If dug up, washed carefully and dried, the roots however, form a first-rate herb for improving the general health and for promoting quiet sleep and a good complexion. It is also a specific for urinary complaints.

When grown deliberately as a useful infusion-making herb, it must somehow be kept out of the cultivated area of the garden as the roots go very deep indeed and can regenerate, even if broken, to form new plants again from the smallest fragment.

*Couch grass*

The rhizomatous roots are knotty and tuberous and should be dug up in early spring and then boiled to release their virtues. The quantity needed is from 2-4 oz (50-100g) in a quart (about 1 litre) of water which should be boiled down to 1 pint (575ml). The strong extract should be bottled and given in ½-2 teaspoonful doses, in water.

**CRESS*** (*Lepidium sativum*). Garden cress, so often grown indoors as baby plants for winter salads and eaten before it grows to maturity, is now thought to have great antiseptic and, of course, antiscorbutic powers, as well as providing the eater with a measure of antibiotic substance.

A strong infusion made from a small handful of washed, crushed mature plants, which are simple to grow from seed in the garden, can be used as a lotion for small wounds which stubbornly refuse to heal. Seed can be bought from any garden centre or gardening shops.

**CUCUMBER*** (*Cucumis sativus*), Cukes, Cowcumber. Although cucumbers provide us with delicious, even though sterile, unripe fruits for salads and sandwiches, pickling and soup-making, they also can be used as a soothing lotion. They should be squeezed or mashed in a blender (or preferably juiced) to make an excellent complexion lotion and the result used daily to 'improve the spotty skin' or for removing all kinds of blemishes.

Juiced cucumber, with equal parts of glycerin and rose-water (obtainable from some chemists and herbal extract suppliers) added to it, makes a soothing lotion for chapped hands and 'ragged' lip.

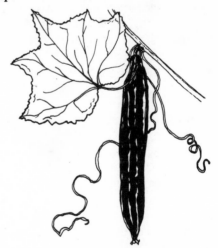

*Cucumber*

**CUDWEED, MARSH** (*Gnaphalium uliginosum*), Cotton Weed, Everlasting Herb. A small downy-leaved wildflower with dingy yellow flowers, which appear in clusters in late summer.

*Cudweed (marsh)*

This plant is only included here because of its extraordinary good properties for making either an excellent ulcer-healing mouth wash and gargle or a herbal tea for treating quinsy. Both gargle and tea are made by pouring 1 pint (575ml) of boiling water over 1 oz (25g) of the herb. The latter should be taken in wineglassful doses, three times a day.

**CUMIN** (*Cuminum cyminum*). Cumin is one of the oldest-known of the culinary spices. It came, originally, from the East but it is also grown, now, in mediterranean countries.

The seeds can be bought from health stores, or from shops where Indian and Chinese foods and cooking ingredients are sold. It might be worth planting a few in a pot of soil and seeing if they germinate. The plants need a sheltered place and plenty of warmth if they are to go to seed and if the seeds are to ripen.

Although, basically, Cumin seeds were used for flavouring, particularly

*Cumin*

for curry, this is a carminative or 'wind-breaking' herb, for 'those with lazy flatulent digestions'. A tea can be made, in the usual way, from the crushed seeds.

**DANDELION** (*Taraxacum officinale*), Hare's Lettuce, Clock-flower, Devil's Milk-pail, Horse Gowan, including many delightfully vulgar country names describing the effect of over-indulgence caused by eating too many of the young leaves and flower buds of Dandelion.

This extremely common and well-known wildflower probably has earned more popular names than any other. Its glaringly golden 'miniature sun' flowers shine out from spring hedge-banks and fields. They are collected to make wines but also make a useful herbal infusion which should be drunk very sparingly.

Put *a few* flower-heads, together with a leaf or two, into green salads early in the year to increase the appetite, if it is jaded after a long cold winter, or after weeks of debilitating poor health.

Dandelion leaves can be chopped and eaten raw and a tea made from them, without flowers, is useful as a slimming, diuretic and slightly laxative drink.

In the autumn, as the leaves start dying back, Dandelion roots can be dug, well-scrubbed and dried in a very slow oven before being ground down to make Dandelion coffee. A teaspoonful of the resulting powdery remains, which should be kept in a tightly lidded jar, makes an excellent winter drink if it is added to a cupful of hot milk and water and sweetened with a little honey.

Dandelion wine can be made simply by pouring a gallon of boiling water over a gallon of the flowers. Stir well and leave it to stand — after covering the top over with a thick cloth — for three days. Stir occasionally during this time and at the end of three days, strain and boil the remaining liquid for half an hour with 5 pints (3 litres) of loaf sugar, some chopped ginger and the rind from a couple of small oranges. Strain and allow it to cool. Add a teaspoonful of yeast on a small bit of toast and cover it all up again and leave for a couple of days or until it has stopped fermenting. Do not bottle for several months but keep in a tightly corked cask in a cool place.

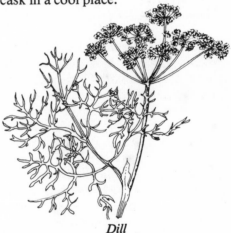

*Dill*

**DILL\*** (*Anethum graveolens*). Dill is probably one of the herbs that were introduced into Britain and Northern Europe by the Romans. It is an attractive plant to grow in gardens but needs plenty of space as it often enjoys good garden soil and makes a tall, fine 'back of the border' herbaceous plant.

The ripe seeds can be collected and kept in a freezer or, if carefully dried first, in lidded jars in a dry place. The

*Dandelion*

leaves, for flavouring purposes, can also be dried.

Dill tea, used for centuries for fretful infants, is a carminative or wind-dispeller. It is made by infusing a small teaspoonful of ripe seed in a cupful of boiling water and leaving it to stand for a few minutes. A saltspoonful of honey or raw brown sugar improves the flavour.

The young leaves of Dill improve the flavour of soups and fish. They are delicious if chopped with salads, parricularly if cucumber is being used, as they seem to bring out and improve its delicate flavour.

**ELDER\*** (*Sambucus nigra*), Boon-tree, Judas-tree, Dog-tree, Tea-tree, Scaw. Elders are also known as Pipe-trees and Whistle-trees, since their pith-filled twigs used often to be hollowed out to make pea-shooters and whistles by country children.[1]

The tree is very widely-known and grows wild in Britain and Europe. It is frequently sown by birds which eat the ripe, black berries and pass the seed through their intestines and out onto fresh soil in other places, together with all the other unwanted parts of their food.

Teas can be made from Elder leaves, flowers and berries. Mild Elder-leaf tisane, or even Elder leaf-bud tisane, have a reputation for acting as a spring tonic.

A strong infusion made from fresh, young leaves, is often used by gardeners who hate using toxic chemical sprays, as a spray to get rid of plant pests. It is said to be especially effective against blight in fruit trees and against the aphis. It is also excellent for watering compost heaps and, when applied as a fine spray, for deterring caterpillars from eating seedling plants.

Elderflower tisane is delicious and most refreshing to drink. The flowers need to be picked when they are at their best, just as the flower-buds are wide open, as soon as they smell fragrant and not after the bees have collected all the nectar. They are also best used when freshly picked, although it is per-fectly possible to dry them. For external lotions, Elderflower water, is made like the tea, with 1 oz (25g) of herb to 1 pint (575ml) of boiling water. It is excellent for a skin-wash as it is stimulating and astringent in effect. The dried flowers, strangely enough, seem to produce a more potent (though not as deliciously fragrant) result than an infusion of fresh blossom.

Internally, Elderflower infusions should only be taken in small doses

*Elder*

---

[1] This can be dangerous, though, as there is poison in the woody sap.

and if a cupful is drunk before breakfast, it is said to increase all aspects of bodily and mental health.

Elderberries can be made into wine, or syrup or tea. The latter can be drunk hot to reduce a fever (flavoured with lemon and sugar or with peppermint) and to provoke a sweat. Qualified herbalists also used it in a sweat-producing mixture with Yarrow.

**ELECAMPANE\*** (*Inula helenium*), Horseheal, Wild Sunflower. This huge plant grows wild, although it is not thought to be a native plant in Britain. Possibly, it was brought back with the Crusaders after they had found that it made an invaluable veterinary remedy for their horses.

It is a very tall, coarse-leaved plant with heads of big yellow daisy-like flowers and its roots used to be picked to be candied and eaten as a sweet, rather on the same lines as Angelica stems.

It can certainly be grown from root cuttings in large gardens and needs a shady, damp situation where it can be decorative.

Elecampane tea, for humans, is made from the dried root which is obtainable from herbalists. It is almost a herbal specific for bronchitis and other hard, dry coughs, and is now thought to be strongly antibacterial.

**EVENING PRIMROSE\*** (*Oenothera biennis*), Moth-blossom, Night-opener. As the old country names show, this wild, yellow-flowered plant really only opens at night. The flowers then have a delicious fragrance.

It can be grown from seed and a few of the young leaves may be added to salads. Evening Primrose's virtues as a tea-maker lie only in the fact that some herbalists find that this plant (which incidentally is not even related to the Primrose) is most useful for asthmatics. It must, however, only be taken if prescribed by a qualified herbalist.

*Elecampane*

*Evening primrose*

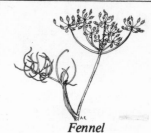

*Fennel*

Common Fennel grows tall and both kinds of Fennel can be obtained as seed from herbal nurseries. They need space in which to grow, so neither is suitable for very small gardens or window-boxes.

The leaves of both Fennels can be used sparingly to flavour fish sauces and soups and they are useful for making a pleasing and carminative drink. This plant also has the reputation of being an appetite increaser as well as a slimming herb, for according to an old herbalist, it makes 'them who are fat grown lean'. It also acts as a stimulant.

Fennel seeds were among those that used to be carried in the pocket to be chewed during boring meetings, services and long public talks.

**FENUGREEK** (*Trigonella foenum-graecum*), Bird's Foot, Classical Greek Clover, Greek Hay-seed. The last of this forage crop's popular names gives a clue to its most familiar use, for it is a most useful green, nitrogenous-aid to the soil and is very widely cultivated. Agricultural experts now recommend that farmers grow it both for its potential as a fodder-plant and as a land-enricher or, in other words, a natural fertilizer.

*Eyebright*

**EYEBRIGHT** (*Euphrasia officinalis*), Casse-lunettes, Peewits, Clear-eye. This wild plant has small white flowers with purple stripes and yellow flecks. It appears in chalky pastures and has always been associated with being helpful for inflammations of the eyes.

A diluted infusion of lotion of the whole herb (which is obtainable already in tincture form from herbal chemists) is superb for clearing the eyes and for strengthening them.

*Eyebright should not be used internally.* It is included here purely as an eye-bathing lotion-maker.

**FENNEL\*** (*Foeniculum vulgare*), Finkle, Seaside Ferny-plant. There are actually two forms of Fennel in cultivation and one with a swollen base, is used as a delightful root-vegetable in Britain and overseas. Both can be grown in gardens and make decorative plants with their extremely finely-divided leaves.

*Fenugreek*

Fenugreek is rich in mineral elements and could be useful as a human as well as an animal food. This was clearly demonstrated when there was a craze in Britain, Europe and the United States for sprouting plants and eating their newly germinating seeds. Fenugreek was then shown to be one of the easiest and pleasantest of all to grow. It is generally thought to be good in salads and sandwiches.

It is another herb with, so far, untested medical potential, but its traditional reputation is extremely high for many different complaints. It is supposed to stimulate the appetite, to provide a quietening and soothing drink, if its seeds are soaked to the point when they begin to swell and are then strained off. This has also been suggested as a mucilaginous stomach-soother.

The soaked seeds themselves are useful for external poulticing lotions which can be used for inflammations such as boils and abscesses.

If a tisane is made from the seeds, or indeed from fresh young shoots, the plant needs to be very fresh as so many of its virtues obviously lie in its vitamin and trace-element content. It can taste a little bitter, but this is easily masked by the addition of a little honey or brown sugar.

It is only very occasionally found truly wild in Britain and grows freely as a native plant on warm shores of the Mediterranean, as well as being cultivated in many countries throughout the world.

*Feverfew*

**FEVERFEW\*** (*Chrysanthemum parthenium*), Batchelor's Buttons, Nosebleed, Midsummer Daisy. Just lately this plant has been much in the public eye as a herb for headaches. It is true that it helps some people, either eaten raw (chopped leaves) or made into a tisane. It can even take away the trial of migraines. But it is not a specific and just as the causes of headaches are legion, it will depend greatly on the cause of the headache as to whether Feverfew helps or not.

It should be remembered that Feverfew can also act as an aperient. Infusions are bitter but should be sweetened with a little honey.

*Fig*

*Figwort*

**FIG\*** (*Ficus carica*). Dried figs, picked in countries that are warmer than those in the Northern Hemisphere, can be soaked and gently boiled to provide a tea which can be made even sweeter with honey, after it has been strained. This acts as a good laxative. Actually, if kept in the refrigerator before drinking, it is absolutely delicious. This is all reminiscent of the 'Syrup of Figs' which was given for any form of constipation in childhood, but which also contains senna and rhubarb extracts.

Diluted juice from fresh green figs, if you are fortunate enough to have a sheltered, warm sunny wall on which to grow them, can be made after the figs have been 'juiced'. *Drink both dried and fresh fig tea with care and very sparingly.*

**FIGWORT** (*Scrophularia nodosa*), Brownwort, Crowdy-kit, Fiddlesticks, Poor Man's Salve. The last of the popular country names describes one of this plant's uses for it is an excellent herb for the skin.

Figwort grows wild in damp and shady places and has a loose spike of small, weirdly-shaped brown flowers that are pollinated by wasps. The whole plant, collected and dried in early summer when it is flowering, is used by herbalists not only for skin troubles, but as a cure for swellings and sprains and muscle-injuries. A twisted or bruised ankle is helped by placing Figwort leaves on it.

Figwort lotion, made from fresh or dried leaves and other parts of the plant, is good to apply to abscesses and less serious skin eruptions, but can help some cases of eczema. It is one of the plants that were first found to alleviate the misery of scrofula and is also still called the Scrofula Plant in parts of

Britain. Another of its traditional names is Carpenters' Herb, from its ability to heal cuts and scratches and bruises that carpenters are inclined to get as they work.

This popular name, though, according to some people, arose because of the plant's four-sided, square stems and either interpretation of the old picturesque name could be true.

**FLAX*** (*Linum usitatissimum*), Mary's Linen Cloth, Linseed. The famous linseed tea, made from the seeds of this plant, that used to be boiled and softened until they formed a gelatinous drink which was then given to horses 'with the cough', seems to be now supplanted in stables by more modern, easier-to-make and administer, veterinary drugs. This tea,

*Flax*

however, still makes a soothing cough cure for humans as it is so demulcent. It is also a useful, harmless drink for sufferers from any urinary complaint. The cooked seeds make useful poultices for festering sores.

*Fumitory*

**FUMITORY** (*Fumaria officinalis*), Lady's Lockets, Wax Dolls, Smoke-plant, God's Fingers and Thumbs. This has always been a much-appreciated little herb of the fields. Even in the fourteenth century, a poet wrote:

> Fumiter is erbe, I say,
> That springyth in April and in May,
> In feld, in town, in yerd and gate
> Where land is fat and good in state.

Fumitory tea is a tonic drink with gentle laxative properties and which purifies the blood. It can also be used externally as a complexion-improver and to help sunburn.

**GARLIC*** (*Allium sativum*), Poor man's Treacle, Ramsons, Mock-lily, Gypsy's Onions, Stink-plant. There can be no doubting the popularity of this common wildflower, for it has such a wide variety of local country names. Some of them are derogatory, because it smells so strong, but others

*Garlic*

are appreciative. 'Treacle', by the way, means a health-giving herb and has an ancient and curious definition through a Greek word which I can only render as 'thiacle'.

Garlic, chopped into stews, casseroles, into salads, sandwiches and added to sauces and other dishes which are improved by its flavour, not only improves the flavour, but is also extremely beneficial. This plant has great antiseptic properties, it rids dogs and cats of intestinal worms and fleas and can be given in capsule form (if they will not take it with their food).

The wild and the cultivated garden Garlic can also be made into a tea. Wineglassesful of the infusion, made in the usual way from fresh or dried material, are said to be helpful to asthmatics. The bulbs, crushed before being infused or lightly simmered, are also believed to be useful for epileptics.

In fact, its devotees regard Garlic almost as a panacea for all ills.

Garlic-takers, who fear having stinking, off-putting breath, can lessen the plant's lingering aroma by afterwards chewing a leaf of fresh Parsley, or by eating and really masticating a raw apple.

**GERANIUM.**
See ROSE GERANIUM.

*Gillyflower*

**GILLYFLOWER*** (*Dianthus caryophyllus*), Clove-pink, Border Carnation, Sweet-as-sugar-flower. Concentrated syrups and infusions made from the petals of these deliciously scented flowers can be used as flavourers. They can also be candied or used to make an unusual and fragrant tisane. Apart from providing such a sweet taste, which slightly resembles cloves, this plant has no special properties. The coloured petals do, however, make a delightful drink.

**GINGER** (*Zingiber officinale*). Ginger, of which the root is such a famous flavour giver, is said to have come originally from the Far East. It is now grown, under cultivation, in Africa and the West Indies and as far west as Jamaica. To add to Ginger's many delights which range from it being obtainable in a crystallized state to that of a sweet syrup, it is also

*Ginger*

*Ginseng*

possible to make a tea or infusion. Pour 1 pint (575ml) of boiling water over only ½ oz (15g) of grated or powdered root to make a useful carminative (digestive and flatulence-dispelling) drink and sip a wineglassful at a time, while it is still hot, before or after meals.

**GINSENG.** The American plant, *Panax quinquefolium,* is now the far more commonly grown and used as the Chinese Ginseng (*Panax pseudoginseng*) is now very expensive and rare. Both have inherited such vernacular names as Livelong, Life Everlasting and Fivefinger Plant and have revitalizing and rejuvenating powers attributed to them.

Certainly Ginseng seems to help some people, giving them improved health and a new lease of life. However, it does not do the same for everyone and there are many disappointments because this herb does not always have an effect.

Ginseng once only grew in China and as the demand for its roots increased, the plant became very scarce. Now it is cultivated in the U.S.A. and even re-imported to China.

Once mature enough to be dug up, the roots are washed, when their irregular shape can be seen. Some resemble the grotesque figure of a little man.

A decoction of the prepared root made as a tea from the dried herb is most beneficial to some who suffer from nervous dyspepsia or to those who might benefit from a tonic and appetite-stimulator and it certainly can sometimes, if drunk first thing in the morning, create a feeling of well-being.

**GOOSEFOOT** (*Chenopodium bonus-henricus*), Good King Henry, Poor Man's Spinach. This is an uncommon wild plant, growing sometimes near villages, possibly as a relic of cultivation. It is only one of the Goosefoot family and one that was chosen for its potential, in the old days, for making a useful 'pot-herb', the other Goose-foots supposedly having poisonous qualities.

A lotion can be made from the leaves, in the usual way of making infusions, which can be used on poultices to cover stubborn and sceptic wounds and ulcers. It has an old reputation of being an excellent healer.

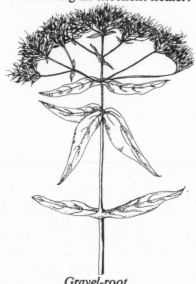

*Gravel-root* .

**GRAVEL-ROOT\*** (*Eupatorium purpuretum*), Joe Pye Weed, Queen-of-the-meadow root, Purple Boneset. This tall American plant was a favourite herb of the Red Indians and like so many that they used, is extremely effective. It is imported into this country and can be bought from herbalists and health stores. Actually, it can also be grown in gardens, where it makes a handsome but space-taking addition to our usual herbaceous borders. It attracts bees and butterflies.

Gravel-root tea is used as a diuretic, a diaphoretic and as an astringent tonic. It is said to be useful to those with chronic urinary troubles and even, as its common name suggests, to be able to disperse 'gravel' or stones.

**GREATER CELANDINE.**
See page 51.

*Ground elder*

**GROUND ELDER** (*Aegopodium podagraria*), Bishopweed, Goutweed, Goatweed, Herb Gerard. This difficult garden weed can also be used as a vegetable but if, as so many gardeners find, it romps too quickly through other plants in a garden, it can also be killed by repeatedly sifting fine wood-ash over it. This, I understand, blocks the leaf pores and so inhibits their growth.

However, if it is growing on a bit of waste ground, Ground Elder makes a useful medicinal herb which can be made into a tea for relieving aching joints. If applied as a skin-wash it is said to subdue an over-ruddy complexion.

**GUELDER-ROSE\*** (*Viburnum opulus*), Whitsun-boss, Cramp Ball, Gaitre-berry, May Rose. This delightful shrub is obtainable in different forms from nurseries. In some, the flowering heads have been cultivated so that all the separate flowerlets have the bigger white outer perianth segments: the result is that the flower-head is full and rounded into a white sphere.

For a herbal drink, Guelder-Rose bark is made into a decoction for a nervine and especially as a relief for those who suffer badly from cramp. *Guelder-Rose berries must be cooked if they are picked for eating.*

*Guelder-rose (wild fruit)*

*Guelder-rose (cultivated form's flowers)*

**HAWKWEED, MOUSE-EARED** (*Hieracium pilosella*). This pretty wild-flower grows on sunny, short-turfed banks and flowers early in the year. Its leaves are softly hairy (but not as rounded as a mouse's ears), and its solitary double-daisy-like flowers, are about the size of a five-pence piece and are a clear lemon-yellow. Their backs, however, often have a reddish tinge. These features make it easy to distinguish from the other, coarser Hawkweeds.

In infusion — made in the usual way, by pouring 1 pint (575ml) of boiling water over 1 oz (25g) of the fresh herb — Mouse-eared Hawkweed has several helpful properties, including that of stopping nose-bleeding if plugs of cotton-wool, soaked in it, are used. An alternative, though rather harsh method, is to sniff the dried and powdered herb up the nostrils.

If intended for drinking, the infusion may well have to be sweetened to make it palatable, but it is an admirable 'provoker of the sweat' and a good tonic. This Mouse-eared Hawkweed has the reputation of being the best of all herbs for whooping cough.

As a lotion, again, an infusion makes a good, soothing application for

*Hawkweed (mouse-eared)*

haemorrhoids, which can be improved, as is sometimes suggested, by gently boiling the plants' leaves in milk.

**HAWTHORN\*** (*Crataegus monogyna*), May, Maybuds, Hagthorn (a 'hag' was one of the old names for a witch), Our Lady's Meat, Cuckoobuds, Bread and Cheese Tree. There are so many country names still used to describe this well-known little tree, which seems to grow almost all over the world, and this indicates the extent of the affection that country people have for it, as well as giving a few clues about how useful it has been found to be in traditional old remedies.

Modern herbalists seem to favour the plant very highly too and it is chiefly used as a heart tonic. Hawthorn tinctures can be obtained from herbal chemists and is sometimes given in the dosage of ten drops in a little water before meals as a gentle cordial tonic and sometimes added to tinctures from other herbs to augment its own virtues.

Country people, when out for a walk, still pick the leaf buds while they are tender and young and eat them. But

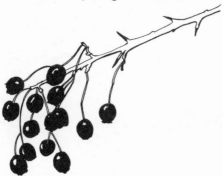

*Hawthorn (fruits)*

care must be taken not to pick and eat any wild plants that grow where they may now be polluted. If clean, however, the buds are quite pleasant to chew.

**HEATHER** (*Calluna vulgaris*), Ling. In northern parts of Britain, and in Scotland particularly, country people used to add the tips of flowering shoots of heather to herbal drinks and beers to purify the blood. The resulting infusion, when heather was used alone, was also used as a cosmetic herb to improve the complexion and to rid it of freckles. 'Spotty adolescents' were made to drink a daily mugful of Heather tea.

*Heather*

**HEDGE GARLIC** (*Alliaria petiolata*), Jack-by-the-hedge, Garlic Mustard. This wild plant, one of the first to appear in spring, produces stems of green leaves topped by small white flowers. It has been used as a vegetable and, if picked young enough, can be tender and taste faintly of garlic.

*Hedge Garlic*

Personally, though, I would not recommend it! Young leaves are pleasanter eaten raw and chopped up in salads. A lotion made from the whole fresh plant, 1 oz (25g) to 1 pint (575ml) of boiling water, makes a soothing poultice for joints that are 'full of the screws', as country people used to call rheumatism. It is also a useful herb for poulticing nagging neuralgic pains.

**HOPS\*** (*Humulus lupulus*). It is the female flowers of the Hop that are picked and dried to be used in the preparation of beer. They are also used by herbalists to make a calming, sedative tea (and used to stuff pillows for the same purposes), which if drunk first thing in the morning, can help a hangover headache.

Hop tea, made in the usual way, is good for several purposes. It is a tonic

*Hops*

and an alterative, and aids the appetite. However, it is also very bitter and is improved by the addition of some honey (only a little) or raw brown sugar.

Externally, used as a lotion, it is often successful in alleviating pain from hot, swollen joints and it can also be used as a poultice for boils, as well as for deep bruises.

**HYSSOP\*** (*Hyssopus officinalis*). Hyssop is a well-known garden herb and is also one of the Holy herbs: 'Purge me with Hyssop and I shall be clean', the scriptures say. It occasionally grows in a naturalized state on old abbey ruins. Its small, purple-blue flowers are a delightful colour and it is possible to picture medieval ladies trying to match their silks to make their tapestries and other embroideries 'as blue as true hyssope'.

Hyssop infusions promote expectoration, act as a sweat-maker (diaphoretic), a tonic and are 'grateful to a feeble stomacke'. They can be exceptionally helpful to cases of stubborn catarrh. An old cookery book gives this recipe: 'Infuse a quarter of an ounce of dried hyssop flowers in a pint of boiling

*Hyssop*

water for ten minutes; sweeten with honey, and take a wineglassful three times a day, for debility of the chest. It is also considered a powerful verm-ifuge.' (A vermifuge is an internal, usually intestinal, worm-expeller).

**JASMINE.** An exotic, Chinese jasmine is used to make Jasmine tea and I know of no other purpose in prescribing it than that of the sheer delight in drinking it. The flowers are frequently mixed with those of China Tea but to those who do not normally drink China or Indian tea, plain Jasmine-flower tea is vastly preferable. It can be difficult to obtain and must be asked for, carefully.

**JUNIPER** (*Juniperus communis*), Melmot berries, Horse-saver, Bastard-killer. Juniper has an old reputation as an abortient. However, taken oc-casionally and with care, a tea made from the dried fruits is often helpful, using ½ oz (15g) to 1 pint (575ml) of

*Juniper*

boiling water, as a diuretic as well as a carminative herb. Sheep are said to be fond of nibbling off the blue-black berries from Juniper bushes that grow on chalk downland and certainly rabbits appear to seek them out. It was Juniper, together with other smaller chalk-loving plants, that was said to help to give the Southdown lamb its delicious flavour.

**KNAPWEED, GREATER** (*Centaurea scabiosa*). Large Hardhead, Churls-heads, Bottleweed, Horse-knobs. This is a beautiful wildflower which is common in hedgerows and at field edges in Britain, particularly in the south. It attracts many bees and butter-flies to its shaggy, deep-magenta flower-heads and packs of goldfinches alight on its fruiting heads to take the seeds. These seeds can be used to make

*Greater Knapweed*

a lotion in which to soak a pad to stop nosebleed.

**KNOTGRASS** (*Polygonum aviculare*), Ninety-knot, Sparrow-tongue, Cowgrass. This rather insignificant weed seems to grow all over the world. It creeps over country paths, its red

*Knotgrass*

stems being as thin as wire except at the joints, which are enlarged, hence many of its traditional, country names, including the most common of all, Knotgrass, and also Centinode.

Its seeds are sought by finches and the whole herb is collected by herbalists for its astringent properties. Externally, an infusion is used as a styptic, and as a dressing for dirty wounds. Internally, Knotgrass tisane can be used to help those with the diarrhoea and, strangely enough, for 'comforting the nerves and tendons'.

The herb should be gathered just as it comes into flower if it is to be used for medicinal purposes.

**LAVENDER\*** (*Lavandula angustifolia*). This well-known aromatic herb is too familiar to need any description. Its fragrance, when fresh, is delightful. Personally, I do not think that the scent is as attractive after it has been dry for some time, as it goes slightly musty.

*Lavender*

The plant is native to the mediterranean region but grows and indeed flourishes in gardens in Britain and other cool parts of Europe. It is also cultivated in Australia, as are many of our other old herbs.

Lavender oil is used to make perfumes which then scent many different cosmetic products. This oil is expensive to produce as many flowers-heads are needed for the distillation of a small quantity of perfume and it is, therefore, extremely dear to buy. A few drops, however, go a long way. The old herbalist, Gerard, used to recommend that they 'that have the palsy . . . profiteth much, if they are anointed with Lavender oil and Olive oil', which is interesting in view of the recent interest in Aromatherapy (see *Useful Addresses* for suppliers of aromatic oils) in which natural oils are used on the skin with much benefit.

Lavender tisane, in which only a few flower-heads are infused in boiling water and drunk *in small quantities occasionally,* is delightful and relieves extreme fatigue and acute physical exhaustion.

**LEMON** (*Citrus limonia*). The wonderful fruit of the Lemon tree is useful in so many ways. The juice takes the place of vinegar in many households and is especially useful to those who suffer from over-acid stomachs. In fact, it is not only the fruit-juice that is useful, for the rind or peel, thinly pared, can be candied in sugar, to add flavour to cakes, biscuits and puddings, and to decorate them, too.

*Lemon*

Lemon tea, prepared by adding some lemon juice to *cold* water, should preferably be drunk unsweetened. Of course, many delicious forms of lemonade can be produced and cooled for summer drinks and other flavouring, such as Mint, only add to the delight.

A few sips of lemon tea are often enough to stop a stubborn attack of hiccups and can help those with a fever.

**LEMON BALM\*** (*Melissa officinalis*), Sweet Balm, Bee Balm and Honey Balm. Everyone can grow this plant. Indeed, many people grow more than they want in gardens, for it is a spreader and pops up all over the place. If it is controlled, however, it is a good garden plant as bees love it and a few old country-people have actually called it 'Welcome-home-bees', adding that if planted near hives, beekeepers will never lose their stock.

The deeply-veined, heart-shaped leaves can be used in the usual way to make a refreshing and carminative drink, especially for those with a high

*Lemon Verbena*

*Lemon Balm*

temperature, as this herb also has diaphoretic virtues. An infusion needs to stand for about fifteen minutes and then should be strained and allowed to cool.

As a tea, for sheer delight, it should be sweetened with honey.

**LEMON VERBENA*** (*Aloysia triphylla*). This is a tender shrub when planted in Britain and needs winter protection, as hard frosts kill it. If grown in the shelter of a south-facing wall, however, and covered up carefully in late autumn with dry bracken fronds, it can survive and give many years of pleasure through its diffusive scent.

A tisane, made by pouring 1 pint (575ml) of boiling water onto, say, ten leaves, always causes exclamations of delight from those who have never tasted it before. Some people, who normally like their tea sugared, prefer it with a little honey added.

The leaves, picked in high summer, dry very easily in a warm place and can then be stored for winter use. Actually, Lemon Verbena 'tea' is also said to be useful as an expectorant.

**LETTUCE, WILD** (*Lactuca virosa*). This uncommon wild plant is not easy to find and if the herb is to be used for making an infusion, it should be bought dried and prepared for use from a herbalist or health shop.

Wild Lettuce tea is sometimes prescribed as a mild sedative and it can be most effective for sleepless people, but be careful not to let its juice get near the eyes as it is an irritant. Also be *sure* of its accurate identification.

*Lettuce (wild)*

**LILY-OF-THE-VALLEY\*** (*Convallaria majalis*), May Lily, Rabbits' Ladders, Our Lady's Tears. This enchanting little flower grows in a naturalized state in a few woods, as well as in our gardens. It is, though, really a garden plant.

*Lily-of-the-Valley*

As a plant for making a herbal drink, it must be used with care and *it is important that it should only be used if prescribed by a medical herbalist.* The dried flowers can be bought in specialist herbal chemists, or from herbalists, if necessary.

It is a useful plant, when used correctly, for making a cheering, heart tonic. A tisane made solely from the open flowers has an enchanting flavour, but really ought not to be taken for this alone.

**LINSEED.**
See FLAX.

**LIME\*** (*Tilia cordata*), Little Linden Tree, Winged or Wind flowers. These Lime trees grow sparingly, as wild trees, all through the Northern Hemisphere and produce a mass of perfect, scented flowers in high summers. The flowers are green, but they have yellow anthers and they are all attached to pale green bracts — hence their name of 'winged' flowers. The bract, in actual fact, acts as a wing and they are blown about to disperse the fruit far from their parent trees.

When they are at their best these small-leaved Lime flowers attract bees from all around, and this is when they should be gathered. They smell strongly of honey and once this scent fades, they must be regarded as being too old to use. *Never try to use them once they begin fading.*

Lime tisane is a great favourite, possibly the best-known and loved of all the herbal drinks, particularly in Europe. Not only is it bliss to drink, but it has so many soothing, stress-relieving and fatigue-lifting properties, as well as being helpful to the digestion. It is one of the herbs that are effective really quickly and its ability to relieve nervous-headache must be tested to be believed. It is also useful for those who find it hard to sleep.

*Lime*

A lotion made from Lime flowers is good for spots, if dabbed actually on the spots themselves. It is also excellent to use (made stronger than for internal purposes) as a hair tonic and is said to lighten fair hair if it is regularly applied after the final rinse.

**LIQUORICE** (*Glycyrrhiza glabra*). Liquorice root is imported from warmer countries, although it was once cultivated in Britain. It would be interesting to try it again, in gardens, as the old herbalists tell of ways that it was cultivated and 'thereof good profit was made'.

*Liquorice*

Liquorice tea, which is an infusion of the root, is now being used by qualified herbalists as an excellent drink for those with stomach ulcers: it is a soothing, emollient and demulcent herb. It is also used for colds and coughs and can be sweetened with honey or a little black molasses, although it is already sweet if properly harvested and dried.

*Lovage*

**LOVAGE\*** (*Ligusticum scoticum*). This big herb grows wild in only a few places in Britain; for example, on cliffs in Scotland, but it is easy to cultivate in gardens, as long as there is room for it. It is used as a culinary herb for its flavour, which often seems reminiscent of Angelica plus a strong taste of Celery.

The roots, fresh leaves and seeds are employed for medicinal purposes. Lovage tea has a strong flavour which some find most pleasant and is a wind-dispeller as well as a slight stimulant. It also makes a good gargle when cold.

**LUNGWORT\*** (*Pulmonaria officinalis*), Jerusalem Cowslip, Soldiers and Sailors, Joseph and Mary. This flower is occasionally found growing wild but is a common garden plant. It

*Lungwort*

*Marigold*

flowers very early in the year, its flowers starting as a dull salmon pink and changing as they age to blue. This, of course, is the reason for some of its double country names.

Judging by the number of popular, traditional names, this must always have been a popular herb. It was said to be good for the lungs and to be 'signed' to that effect (see section on the 'Doctrine of Signatures', page 36).

It is mucilaginous and a tea made from the leaves 1 oz (25g) to 1 pint (575ml) of boiling water — is often helpful to sufferers of persistent coughs. The young leaves, chopped in salads, make a pleasing addition to salads when 'green-stuff' is scarce.

**MARIGOLD\*** (*Calendula officinalis*), Mary's Gold, The Sun's Gold, Bees'-love, Oculis Christi. The large number of common names for this herb point to the fact that it has been a favourite for a long time. Marigolds are garden annuals with wide, orange, single or double flower-heads and are decorative and easy to grow. Seeds can either be collected and saved from year to year or can be bought, but now that different species of *Tagetes* (or French or African Marigolds) are so popular, it is important that the English Marigold, or *Calendula* are grown for future lotion-making.

For this purpose, Marigold flowers and buds provide one of the most valuable of all herbal infusions. The plant has antiseptic and quick-healing virtues and is safe to use externally on all wounds and ulcers. Tincture of Marigold can be obtained from herbal chemists and should always be kept in an easily available place in the house as a few drops in half a cupful of water quickly takes the pain out of burns, scalds, insect bites and stings, as well as acting as a styptic to stop bleeding from deep knife-cuts. Infusions made from fresh Marigolds also serve this purpose.

Marigold petals and tender young leaves should be used, but the resulting

# ALPHABETICAL LIST OF TEA-MAKING PLANTS    81

infusion *should not be taken internally*. The fresh petals can be used safely, in small numbers, to brighten salads or to float on soups, especially vichyssoise or green cucumber summer soups. A few young leaves can also be used in green salads. The juice, directly from the leaves, if they are quickly rubbed together in the hands, also rapidly soothes insect stings and bites.

**MARJORAM*** (*Origanum onites*), Pot Marjoram, Sweet or Swete Margerome. Marjoram has been grown in herb gardens for centuries and has an old reputation of being one of the best aromatic and flavouring herbs. Even modern wildflower text books refer.often to its culinary uses.

It is a perennial and closely related to the Wild Marjoram (*Origanum vulgare*) and is obtainable in the form of

*Marjoram*

young plants from many herb nurseries. It grows particularly well in sheltered places, in hot sunny borders, or containers in gardens. The Wild Marjoram grows on chalk and limestone soil in this country and Northern Europe. It is getting scarce now as so much of the old turf has been ploughed up to make fields for the cultivation of cereal crops. Actually, the flavour of the wild plant is not as good as that from *Origanum onites* and it must be clearly understood, now that conservation of our wild plants is so essential, that they should not be picked, dug up or even have their seeds collected because so many of our wild plants are having difficulty in surviving.

'Swete Margerome' used to be used for a wide variety of domestic purposes. It was one of the ingredients of beeswax furniture polish, used to protect against woodworm. It also kept flies, fleas and moths away. It was a vital ingredient of washing and toilet-waters that 'sweetened the person' and was put, fresh or dried among stored clothes and rubbed down into powder to 'rubbe gently into wigges that be waiting to go onto the head'.

Infusions of the herb, made by pouring 1 pint (575ml) of boiling water over a small handful of leaves or young branch-tips can still be used advantageously, when cool enough, for a hair-rinse. They are also soothing for sprains if a generous layer of surgical wool is soaked in the solution and then bandaged firmly into place. Hot 'Margerome-water', held in the mouth, while the temperature is as high

*Marjoram (knotted)*

as is bearable, was said to 'ease the toothache'.

For internal use, a tisane made in the usual way in the proportion of a heaped teaspoonful of fresh or dried leaves infused in 1 pint (575ml) of boiling water, makes a pleasant and carminative remedy for 'they who be windy'. It should be sipped, while still hot and a wineglassful after meals is generally enough. This is thought to have mild tonic properties and, if taken cold, can be helpful and easily digested in feverish conditions.

**MARSHMALLOW\*** (*Althaea officinalis*), Velvet-leaf, Mallards, Schloss Tea, Mortification Root. This wildflower grows in places near the sea and is one of our most beautiful native plants. Clumps of it line a few shores and some tidal inlets and rivers, as long as they are saline. This tall, handsome plant grows in stands that resemble shrubs but is only a herbaceous peren-

nial with soft, hairy leaves that look as though they might have been dusted in flour. The small, pale-pink, hollyhock-like flowers open in high summer.

It is another herb with a very old country reputation for its demulcent and emollient virtues. It was also used as a pot herb, or vegetable; the young stems used to be picked and cooked fresh, or pickled. There would be a more acute shortage than there is already of this plant, if this were still to be done and it is as well that the roots, which were the original source of supply for making 'comfits and candies' (called, of course 'Marshmallows'), were still to be sought for this purpose. Sweet-manufacturers now have other substitutes.

Cultivated Marshmallow plants are obtainable from some herb-growing nurseries and are easy to grow in gardens. They are perennial so, once planted, will come up year after year, but need to be kept trimmed right back in the autumn. It is also possible, though slower, to raise them from seed.

*Marshmallow*

Professional herb-growers supply herbal pharmacists with leaves and roots for use as simples or in compound mixtures to help to soothe coughs and colds. Packets of dried leaves are available for tisane-making and some herbal practitioners prescribe the infusion for those with kidney complaints.

Externally, a lotion made from fresh or dried leaves — 1 oz (25g) to 1 pint (575ml) of boiling water makes a cleansing complexion tonic. Used for poulticing, this liquid acts as a drawing agent and the leaves themselves, steeped in a little boiling water, then placed between gauze and wrung out to remove the water and applied to 'inflammations of the skin, such as boils, carbuncles and abscesses' act as spectacular means of bringing these unpleasant excrescences to a head. Once the septic matter has been drawn out, the flesh will heal completely.

**MATÉ** (*Ilex paraguayensis*), Paraguay Tea, Jesuits' Tea, Brazil Tea, Yerba Maté. This is a true herbal tea that many people have tried at one time or another. The dried leaves, picked from a South American species of Oak, have to be imported and packets of already prepared Maté Tea can be bought in most health stores and delicatessens.

*It is important always to remember to drink freshly-made Maté* for it goes black and bitter if it stands.

When it is freshly made, as well as having a delightful, smoky flavour, Maté tea is good for you! It has several outstanding and helpful virtues. For

*Maté*

instance, as it is so satisfying, a cupful of Maté can take the place of a fattening snack, and so help slimmers.

It is also slightly soporific if sipped at bedtime, being soothing to the nerves, but it acts as a tonic too and, when taken in the daytime, can help one to think more clearly. It has even been recommended by some herbalists as the drink particularly useful for students engaged in examination-taking.

**MEADOWSWEET** (*Filipendula ulmaria*), Queen-of-the-meadows, Bridewort, Dollof, Lace-makers-herb. This plant grows wild in Britain and Europe in marshy meadows and also along dikes and sometimes railway-banks. It is beautiful in the summer, with its clusters of creamy flowers and red stems and darkish-green compound leaves.

A tisane made from the flowering-heads, the young leaves and branch-tips of the plant before the flower-buds have opened, is pleasant and extremely

*Meadowsweet*

beneficial to those who suffer from acidity. It is also said to make the heart 'gladde and merrie'. People who consume it frequently tell me that a small spoonful of honey makes it even pleasanter to drink, but I know others who prefer its 'herby', flavour plain.

Bees love the flowers and, as they smell so sweet, they are probably rich in nectar. Cattle leave the plant alone in the fields because, one imagines, the older leaves and tough stems, in contrast to the fragrance of the young plant and flowers, both smell and taste of disinfectant. 'Just like carbolic!', my son once said.

**MINTS\*** (*Mentha* sp.). There are many Mints that are easily cultivable in gardens and most of them are rampageous spreaders and should be grown in a confined space. Some gardeners plant them in old bottomless buckets or in tubs or big pots. The young shoots and older leaves are extremely useful for culinary purposes and can be picked and dried for future use, or picked and put into polythene bags, in small quantities, for the deep-freeze.

For making teas, which have good carminative purposes, Peppermint is often chosen, but there are other Mints which are also helpful for indigestion. Hot Mint tea is wonderful for 'wind-breaking' and, according to an old country neighbour of mine, brings up 'the belches a treat'.

The Mints have virtues as cosmetic skin-improvers if used as external lotions. Mint, added to ordinary tea, or steeped in whisky and hot water, then left to cool, makes a simple Mint Julep. An infusion of Mint, made in the same way as a tea — 1 oz (25g) of herb to 1 pint (575ml) of boiling water — makes a good hair-rinse and is said to be a good treatment for scurf. As a mouth-wash the infusion is credited with being 'most excellent for sore gums and tongue' and the leaves, dried and

*Mint*

crumbled, often used to be used instead of toothpaste for whitening the teeth.

Dried Mint can be used sparingly in sweet-herb pillows to encourage restful sleep. It can also be used instead of less pleasant moth-repellants. How useful the Mints are!

Here is a short list of some of the Mints that are easy to grow in gardens:

Spearmint, or Green Mint (*Mentha spicata*).
Apple-mint, or Round-leaved Mint (*Mentha rotundifolia*).
Peppermint (*Mentha x piperita*).
Pennyroyal (*Mentha pulegium*).

There are several others and which you choose will depend upon your preference of flavour. They are usually listed in the catalogues of herb growers.

## MOCCASIN FLOWER, YELLOW
(*Cypripedium pubescens*), Yellow Lady's Slipper Orchid. This American plant looks almost too beautiful when

*Moccasin-flower (yellow)*

seen growing, ever to think of picking it as a useful 'tea'-making herb. However, it is grown commercially in the States, just for this purpose and can be bought already dried and prepared in Britain and in Europe. However, *it must only be used if a doctor or medical herbalist prescribes it.* Properly used, it can be a most helpful sleep-inducing herb, particularly useful for some patients in a nerve-strained, almost hysterical condition.

*Mugwort*

## MUGWORT (*Artemisia vulgaris*),
Apple-pie, Mugger, Smotherwood, Old Uncle Harry, Sailors' Tobacco, and plenty of other country names — some of them very crude. Mugwort is a wayside weed and is common. It can be strikingly beautiful for a short time while it is in fresh flower and the flower-spikes look all 'silver and gold'. But for the rest of the summer, this plant is not attractive as it grows tall and lolls over, and also accumulates roadside dust.

It is useful as a tea-making herb because the leaves can be gathered when they are at their best and used fresh, or dried, in the usual way — 1 oz (25g) to 1 pint (575ml) of boiling water — to make a good stimulating tonic with special properties which relieve nausea.

Mugwort is one of the herbs associated with St John and should, therefore, be at its best at midsummer for his festival. It is supposed to keep fleas and moths 'and other evils' away.

**MULBERRY*** (*Morus nigra*). Mulberry trees are thought to have been introduced into Britain by the Romans. They are interesting garden trees for, in common with the Figs and Walnuts, they are never supposed to come into leaf until all chance of frost is past.

The ripe fruit can be made into wine. It can also be employed to make a laxative tea which should be sweetened with honey or brown sugar. Mulberry juice can be used as a natural colouring for home-made drinks and jellies.

*Mulberry*

*Mullein*

**MULLEIN** (*Verbascum thapsus*), Hag's Tapers, Our-Lady's-flannel, Aaron's Blanket, Aaron's Rod, Duffle, Blanket Herb, Cuddy, Hare's Beard.

A famous botanist, Sir Edward Salisbury, who was Director of the Royal Botanic Gardens at Kew in Surrey after the Second World War, was extremely interested in old traditional country names for wildflowers. He once made a list of all those used, in various localities, for this plant and came to the conclusion that the wild Mulleins had more picturesque, popular names than any other wildflower.

The flowers and the leaves are still gathered by country people to make external lotions and fomentations for toothache and facial neuralgia.

Herbalists also use the flowers for an infusion both for cramp and for gout, taking a wineglassful three times daily, before meals.

**MUSTARD, WHITE\*** (*Sinapsis alba*), Gold Dust. Mustard, like Cress, provides us with most helpful green salad during the coldest, darkest months of the year. The seed can be germinated very easily indoors, in pots, foil trays or even on dampened sponges. Mustard seeds can be 'sprouted' in lidded waterless jars, which should be rinsed out, to keep them damp, at least once a day. The very young growing plants can then be eaten whole, two or three days after they start to grow.

Dry Mustard seeds can be used to make a tea which is good for bronchitis and bad coughs. This infusion should not be made too strong or it will act as an emetic, but a coffee-spoonful of seed to ½ pint (275ml) of boiling water can be used and then tried by sipping it slowly from a wineglass.

*Mustard*

**MYRRH** (*Commiphora myrrha*). Myrrh is a herb with an ancient reputation and has been described since biblical days when it was used to make incense. The fragrance comes from the plant's resin which exudes out of the bark of a shrub which seldom grows more than eight or nine feet tall. It is still used as a base for some perfumes, in incense and in holy oils and grows in hot, eastern, mediterranean countries, as well as in Africa and India.

Myrrh is not often prescribed by herbalists, but a flavoursome mouthrinse which has healing properties can be useful and the herb is frequently used in toothpastes as it is supposed to be helpful to those who have spongy gums. It is also an internal healer with astringent, stimulating and tonic properties, but it must be used with care as its primary virtue, as a tea-making herb, appears to be 'to stimulate a full and insatiable appetite'.

**NASTURTIUM.**
See WATERCRESS.

**NETTLE** (*Urtica dioica*), Bad Man's Playthings, Hoky-Poky, Jenny-nettle, Sting-leaf. Everyone knows Stinging Nettles, but not everyone realizes what a useful weed and herb they are. They can be picked and lightly boiled, sieved and strained to make a green vegetable when they are young and when other greens are often in short supply. They can be cut down, before they seed and added to the compost heap to make excellent green manure and they can also be used to make wonderful lotions and a tisane.

As lotions for external purposes, an infusion of Nettles — 1 oz (25g) to 1 pint (575ml) of boiling water — can be made and allowed to cool. Nettle tincture can also be bought from herbal chemists and is invaluable, when diluted in the proportion of a teaspoonful to 1 pint (575ml) of cold water for burns, scalds, sunburn, insect stings and as a soother for many skin irritations.

As a tisane, for internal use, made in exactly the same way as a lotion, Nettles can be invaluable to those who suffer from rheumatism. A cupful on waking and then before lunch and supper, can often act like magic. Many rheumatic people will find that, however swollen and sore they are, their distorted joints will often benefit from taking Nettle tea regularly. In some districts, Nettles are actually called 'the arthritick's helper'.

*Oat*

**OATS, WILD** (*Avena sativa*). This weed of arable land, which is such a menace to farmers because the only way in which it can be eradicated is by

hand-pulling, is one of the herbalists' favourites.

Cultivated Oats, of course, have great nutritive value, but an infusion of the whole herb of Wild Oats, used fresh or dried, makes a splendid sedative tea. It is calming and soothing to the nerves and good to take at night, as a sleep inducer. A drink made by pouring boiling water over crushed porridge oats has much the same effect and is nutritious to delicate systems.

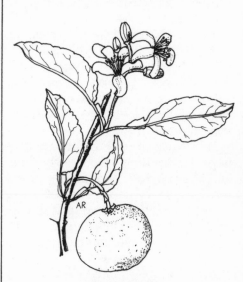

*Orange-buds*

**ORANGE-BUDS** (*Citrus aurantium*), Sweet Orange. The flowers and the flowering buds of this exotic tree are occasionally used by herbalists as another sedative tea-maker. Often too, a few are added by connoisseurs of ordinary tea to improve its fragrance. Orange-bud tea is really one of the herbal teas that can be taken for sheer pleasure.

**PARAGUAY TEA.**
See MATÉ.

*Parsley*

**PARSLEY\*** (*Petroselinum crispum*). This is certainly one of the most commonly grown of all garden herbs. It can be used to make a useful drink when the resulting tisane is slightly sweetened.

An unsweetened tisane made from a teaspoonful of dry Parsley, or a very small handful of fresh leaves, has been known for many generations as a well-tried remedy for those who suffer from urinary troubles. Parsley is a diuretic herb.

**PARSLEY PIERT** (*Aphanes arvensis*), Breakstone, Colicwort. This little wildflower grows on arable land, par-

*Parsley piert*

ticularly where the soil is sandy. It is unrelated to the true Parsley and the whole plant is green, even the very small flowers. Parsley Piert should be gathered as it comes into flower, and can be used either fresh or dry to make a tea.

As the plant is demulcent and also acts as a diuretic, it is usually given to those with chronic urinary difficulties and some inflammation of the bladder. It can also be helpful to those who suffer from biliousness and 'they that be yellow with jaundice'.

*Passion-flower*

**PASSION FLOWER** (*Passiflora incarnata*), Granadilla, Maypops. This American plant is another like the Yellow Mocassin Flower — almost too beautiful to be picked to make a tea! *It should only be used on the advice of a* *doctor or a medical herbalist*, 'for those whom sleep eludes'.

## PELLITORY-OF-THE-WALL (*Parietaria judiaca*), Wall Sage, Billy Beaty.

This is a curious-looking wild plant which grows at the foot, or the top and even out of the sides of old walls. It is related to the Nettle and has been known as a kidney herb for centuries, as well as being a demulcent for soothing sore throats.

It has another use, for making a lotion 'which is comforting to the body' when a strong infusion is made and added to the bath-water. Anyone, however, who suffers from hay-fever should *not* use it. Some concentrated Nettle tea, some strong Rosemary infusion (see page 94) and a good handful of Violet leaves can also be infused and put in the bath to improve the skin. In the old days these ingredients were all added to a bath of hot milk, not water, to provide a 'soaker to ease away fatigue and to beautifie the bodie'.

*Pellitory-of-the-wall*

## PENNYROYAL.
See MINTS.

## PEPPERMINT.
See MINTS.

*Pipsissewa*

## PIPSISSEWA (*Chimaphila umbellata*), Prince's Pine, Rheumatism-weed, Love-in-winter, Ground Holly.

It can easily be guessed from this plant's name that it originated as a helpful herb among North American Indians, who have provided modern herbalists all over the world with so many wonderful remedies. It can be obtained in Britain and Europe, already dried, ready to be made into a tea. As Pipsissewa bark is used, this tea has to be decocted, not infused; that is, boiled according to the directions given on the packet.

It is a diuretic, but it is also a good herb to use as an alterative and a tonic. Sufferers from cystitis find it soothing if their urine is acid and tends to burn when it is being passed. Scientists hope that Pipsissewa may prove to be a helpful plant for diabetics, but as far as I know, this has not yet been proved.

**PLANTAIN** (*Plantago major*), Cuckoo's Bread, Englishman's Foot or White Man's Foot, Snakeweed, Hammerwort. This common weed often appears in gardens as well as growing in the country and in towns all over the world. It seems to have earned itself one of its commonest popular names of Englishman's or White Man's Foot because the natives reckoned that it always seemed to appear wherever colonists trod.

This common Plantain has many virtues as a useful herb. It can be applied externally and is also still prescribed as a helpful tea-making herb — 1 oz (25g) of the plant should be infused in 1 pint (575ml) of boiling water. It should be taken in wineglassful doses three or four times a day, for diarrhoea and haemorrhoids. It has a soothing effect if sipped and held in the mouth, will help toothache. *It is also said to discourage smoking if taken in this way.*

Externally, Plantain is helpful as a styptic, an astringent and a lotion for sunburn. Like a Dock leaf's juice, a crushed leaf or two will take the sting away from nettle burns and insect bites. The juice, when expressed in a juicer, is a wonderful healer for all wounds, even the most stubborn ulcers, as well as being good to make a face-washing lotion, when diluted.

**PRIMROSE\*** (*Primula vulgaris*), Easter Rose, Darling of April, First Rose. Primroses always seem to be the most popular and the most carefully sought of all the British wildflowers. Spring has truly arrived, so some say, when they come out; but this is not strictly true, for most people who live in the country know that a few can often be found in late autumn in sheltered places. However, Primroses somehow epitomize the end of long, dark winters and even act as a tonic if a few flowers are picked and put in sandwiches.

As a medicinal herb, Primrose flowers can be used (if you have them in the garden, but not to be picked wild),

*Plantain*

*Primrose*

to make a sedative tisane. However, *this should not be used unless it is medically prescribed.*

**POT-POURRI TISANE.** If you have a herb garden, it is fun to make a mixture of harmless herbs (but use only up to a teaspoonful) and name it after yourself, or the name of your house, street, village or maybe even your town! Try out mixtures when you are alone, varying the amounts to your taste and then, as you get it tasting deliciously 'herby' and full of fragrance, try some out on your friends.

Start with a Mint leaf or two, then Fennel, perhaps with a snipped-off fragment from a Bay leaf. Then add a few Lemon Verbena leaves, a couple from the tips of Lemon Balm, a small sprig of Elder flowers (when they are in season), a young Borage leaf and some Damask Rose petals, together with a sprinkling of Lavender and Rosemary flowers. This mixture may not please you at all! However, go on experimenting, making your own choice before pouring on the boiling water and letting the miscellaneous tea brew.

A *pot-pourri* tisane can be delightful in summer if it is served cold, with ice and with a medley of attractive 'floaters' (see page 30) including a slice of lemon.

**PRUNES** (*Prunus sp.*). Prunes are dried plums and are grown in mediterranean orchards. The bigger and lusher they are, the more expensive they tend to be.

For tea-making, though, the cheaper ones do nicely. They should be washed and well soaked, then simmered until they are soft in water which has been sweetened with a little brown sugar. When the stones have been carefully removed, the juice and pulp can be put in a blender to make a delicious drink, which can be mildly, or more strongly laxative, according to the amount taken.

*Quassia*

**QUASSIA** (*Picrasma excelsa*), Bitter Wood, Bitter Ash. Quassia tea or lotion is an extremely old remedy for external use as a deterrent for nail-biters! The finger-tips of those who chew their nails or cuticles used to be dipped in solutions made from Quassia wood-chips that had been soaked in water for twelve hours. This made them taste so bitter that it discouraged would-be nail-biters from nibbling. Nowadays, most people would regard this to be a rather out-of-date, drastic treatment.

Used internally, Quassia infusions also seem to be out of date as only a few medical herbalists now prescribe Quassia tea, with added ginger, as a bitter tonic and digestive for 'they who be feeble and thin and have impaired digestions'.

**RASPBERRY** (*Rubus idaeus*), Hindberry, Rasps. Raspberries can be found growing wild in some woods and also in thickets on hills, especially on chalk downs. Their fruit is smaller than that from cultivated canes, but it is delightfully flavoursome and very sweet when ripe.

Two teas can be produced from the Raspberry plant. One produced from the juice of the fruit expressed in a juicer, and sweetened and taken just for sheer delight. This can be frozen in a deep-freeze and kept for future use. The other, from the astringent leaves, which is made in the usual way from fresh or dried young leaves, can be

*Raspberry*

taken by pregnant women, especially towards the end of their pregnancy, to tone up their muscles. *This tea is extremely efficacious* and can be sipped all through the day as it is harmless. It can be sweetened, if preferred, with a little honey or raw brown sugar.

**RHOOIBOSCH** (*Aspalathus linearis*), Red Bush, Red Tea-Making Herb. This traditional true tea may still be better known in South Africa than it is here. But it is now obtainable from some health stores and large delicatessens. The plant belongs to the Pea family, and actually has small yellow flowers but, generally speaking, its red colouring develops after it is gathered, as it is being prepared and processed.

It is a shrub which is native to areas round the Cape, but it is now also being commercially grown in South Africa. The reputation of Rhooibosch tea has always been extremely high, where it was in use, and many 'cures' have been attributed to it, and it is specially recommended for those who suffer from enfeebled digestions. Herbalists, here, recommend it for some forms of gastric derangement, even for young children, with diarrhoea and vomitting after a particular food — most usually, milk. Indeed, it is thought to be most beneficial for children with a milk allergy.

Whatever its other properties, Rhooibosch tea does not contain as much tannin as ordinary tea and it is also rich in vitamin C. Obviously, natives of South Africa, whether black or white, regard it as something of a panacea, but even the most sceptical herbal tea-drinker will give it credit for having some indigestion-relieving and tonic properties.

**RHUBARB** (*Rheum officinale*), Turkish Rhubarb, *not ordinary garden rhubarb.* The use of this plant is very old indeed. It is the roots that are dug up and dried for laxative purposes. It must never be used too strong, or it can be a drastic purgative. So, this plant should always be used with great discretion. Prepared powder of the roots is still given by some herbalists and doctors in very mild doses as a 'soother' for bowel troubles (especially for infants), but it must never be given unless it is medically prescribed.

**RICE** (*Oryza sativa*), Paddy, Nivara, Bras. Rice-water, rather than Rice tea, often makes a useful drink as it is demulcent and has a certain nutritive value for weak and feverish patients. It should be made by boiling washed but unpolished Rice grains until they are soft and then straining them off.

*Rice*

**ROSEMARY*** (*Rosmarinus officinalis*), The Dew of the Sea, Mary's Mantle. This beautiful, fragrant and

*Rosemary*

familiar shrub is one of the most delightful of all plants to have in a garden. It is easy to grow from cuttings which should be 'set', according to folklore, always on Good Friday. (This is the day, too, for sowing Parsley seed!)

Bees love Rosemary flowers and on sunny days both honey-bees and bumble-bees fly to sup from the small, blue blooms.

It has a wide variety of herbal uses. A tea made from the youngest branch-tips can be used occasionally for carminative purposes; it is also believed to have cordial or heart-stimulating virtues. Rosemary infusions should always be made in lidded vessels, as indeed, should many of the herbal tisanes, teas and lotions.

For external use, Rosemary-lotion, or Rosemary-water, needs to be made considerably stronger than the tea for internal use. The latter will be strong enough for most people if made from

½ oz (15g) of chopped herb to 1 pint (575ml) of boiling water, but the 'water', for skin and hair purposes, can have as much as a small handful of the chopped leaves and twig-tips to ½ pint (275ml) of water.

The lotion should be steeped for at least ten minutes; in fact, it can be simmered gently for a few minutes to bring out as much fragrance and oil as possible. When added to the bath-water it makes a most refreshing and invigorating asset for anyone who is tired, but it may be too stimulating for anyone bathing at night. It is also splendid for the hair, so can be used as a final rinse. The actual oil of Rosemary, extracted from the herb, is often used in good hair-preparations as it is thought that it prevents and helps to cure scurf and dandruff and 'to help to grow hair again on bald pates'.

## ROSEMARY WITH HIBISCUS

(*Rosmarinus officinalis* and *Hibiscus sabdariffa*). A prepared herbal tea, already in tea-bags or sachets, is frequently sold in herb shops and delicatessens, made from the two of these herbs. The second plant is an exotic from the East and the West Indies where it is used as a nervine, a stomachic, 'to sweeten the breath' and also as an aphrodisiac. It is used as well to kill insects! It is sometimes known as 'Muck-seed'.

## ROSE* (*Rosa spp.*). Various herbal infusions of great virtue can be made from different species of Roses as well as from different parts of this plant.

*Rose-hip tea* is perhaps the best known and for this, the wild (or briar) Rose is needed. The hips (which are the Roses' fruits) should be gathered when they are red and ripe, at the time, when, in the old days, 'cookes and Gentlewomen do make rose tartes and such like dishes'. But for infusions the hips need gentle and long boiling, then straining and *carefully* sieving. Actually it is such a difficult business sieving out the hairs from the lining of the fruits' valuable walls, that it is far simpler to buy ready-prepared Rose-hip tea from herb shops.

*Rose-hip syrup,* too, is obtainable, but unfortunately it is usually already sweetened. If possible, buy it unsweetened and only add honey which augments and does not detract from its high content of vitamin C.

*Rose-petal tisane* can be made more simply as long as there is a supply of fresh, unwilted Damask Rose flowers. The black-red petals of this highly scented Rose can be eaten, sparingly, in salads and sandwiches as well as being infused to make a tisane (with a little honey), which is said to 'cheer the heart', as Roses were always thought to

*Rose*

*Rose-hips*

be cordial herbs. This may be a link with the Doctrine of Signatures (see page 36), as individual petals are, of course heart-shaped. A delicious conserve can be made with the petals, although a great many need to be gathered as they are so light, but using Malvern water, castor sugar and lemon juice, a small amount of 'jelly' can be produced after a lot of patience!

*Here are the basic instructions:* Boil 1 lb (450g) of Damask Rose petals in 2 pints (about 1 litre) of spring water in a thick-bottomed saucepan, with the lid on. Look at it frequently and stir, to prevent it from sticking.

When the petals are completely softened, remove saucepan from heat and strain the liquid off. Add 4 lbs (about 2kg) of finest sugar (preferably castor) and again boil until the liquid begins to get very syrupy indeed. It takes a long time for the liquid to reduce and the juice of two lemons does help things along a little.

When syrup is thick and does not run off the stirring spoon, pour into already-warmed jars before it sets. Wash saucepan directly it is empty! Rose-petal jelly is extremely tenacious! Scrape the saucepan first, as the deliciousness of this conserve, has to be experienced before understanding that it is worth all the trouble to make.

Doubtless by persisting with the syrup-thickening process, the most exquisite Turkish Delight could be made, but I have never actually tried it.

To go back to Rose-petal tea, before leaving this herb, some home herb-users make it by putting rose-petals (which must be of a fragrant kind) into a flat, clean bowl of Malvern water and leaving it in the sun for a few hours, then straining it, tasting it and adding honey if required, and drinking it by the glassful.

**ROWAN\*** (*Sorbus aucuparia*), Mountain Ash, Quickbeam Tree, Pheasant-berries, Witchwood. This elegant tree grows wild on moors and mountains in Britain and in Europe. It can be grown in gardens, particularly by the superstitious, as it has always been thought to keep the witches away! Actually, it has many associations throughout the ages with folklore.

The delightful orange-coloured berries start ripening in July in southern England. They are extremely acid and are sought by family packs of mistle thrushes which demolish them at a fast rate. They have a high vitamin C content and a few can be gathered, when ripe, for jelly-making (the jelly is

*Rowan*

eaten with game, especially with grouse) or for infusing to make an astringent gargle.

Medical herbalists use a decoction of Rowan bark, which is an astringent for diarrhoea. *It should not be tried without advice from a doctor or a qualified herbalist.*

**SAGE\*** (*Salvia officinalis*). Although there are other herbs that are used for a great number of purposes, it always

*Sage*

seems to me that Sage really does come 'top of the pops'. It has some virtues that other herbs do possess, but it also has many that are unique to it, and it is also easy and decorative to grow in gardens. There are several Sages that can be planted, but perhaps the Red, or Purple Sages look best.

This is another herb with an ancient reputation as one which wards off evil. It was thought to be efficacious 'agaynst the biting of serpents' and the 'dispelling of evill spyrites'.

Sage tea, made in the usual way of pouring 1 pint (575ml) of boiling water over 1 oz (25g) of fresh or dried leaves, can be used as an excellent carminative drink, as a tonic, or a diaphoretic (particularly for feverish colds), or simply as a cheering refreshing drink. It makes a good gargle, especially if cold, and has many other virtues, including that of being a fine hair-dye when the mixture is strong.

Used externally, too, Sage tea was thought to help relieve a headache. It should be cold and a pad of linen 'is soaked therein and gently laid on the forehead', when 'the herb taketh away the agonie of a foul headache'.

A Sage lotion, made in large quantity, can be used for a footbath while it is still hot, for weary, sore and strained ankles and feet. Dabbed onto insect bites and stings, it takes away the heat and itch from them.

**ST JOHN'S WORT** (*Hypericum perforatum*), Bible-flower, Balm-of-the-Warrior or Balm-to-the-Warrior's Wound, Touch and Heal, Penny John,

Holy Herb, and many others. This wildflower grows in all kinds of places in Britain, Europe and in parts of Asia. It seems always to have been regarded as a magic and sacred herb and it flowers at midsummer, near the Feast of St John.

St John's Wort has been used for many purposes, but primarily it is a wound-curer and disinfectant for, used in tincture form (which is available from herbal chemists), it certainly does work like magic to promote healthy healing of deep and shallow wounds. This herb is so powerful in action that it is no wonder that country-people picked bunches of it to put in byres and stables 'to frighten evil spirits and to keep the Devil away'.

Tea made from St John's Wort, made as usual from 1 oz (25g) of herb to 1 pint (575ml) of boiling water, needs sweetening with honey or brown sugar

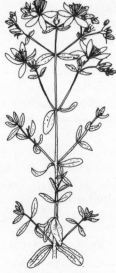

*St John's Wort*

and should only be taken in very small doses of two teaspoonsful to two table-spoonsful at a time. It acts as an astringent, a tonic, a nervine and as an expectorant and was formerly often prescribed for all lung ailments. Country mothers used also to give a few small teaspoonsful at night to small children who were inclined to wet their beds.

Used externally, as a lotion, it is invaluable for all wounds. I have used it for years and can vouch for its unbeat-able efficiency in preventing the dirtiest scratches, cuts and even deep thorn punctures from becoming septic. It is interesting that modern research is proving that St John's Wort has anti-septic properties.

**SARSAPARILLA** (*Smilax ornata*), Rabbit Root, Shot Bush, Wild Sarsa-parilla. This is only one of several Sarsaparillas but it is one that often comes under the title of 'American Sarsaparilla' and one that the Red Indians seem to think of most highly.

The herb is used to make an alter-ative, soothing and slightly diaphoretic tea which is believed to be wonderful for promoting healthy tissue-growth for both internal and external ulcers and wounds. It is also used, externally, as a skin-wash for shingles.

The powdered root can be bought from some herbal chemists with in-structions for its use.

**SASSAFRAS\*** (*Sassafras officinale*), Sassafrax. Parts of the root of this plant, as well as the bark and pith, are

*Ṣassafras*

employed in the preparation of this famous drink, known as American Sassafras Tea, or Saloop, which used even to be sold in the streets of London earlier this century. It was bought from stalls and taken as a stimulant, possibly to help cure hangovers.

It is known to be a mild blood purifier and helps those with feverish symptoms, because of its diaphoretic properties. It makes an aromatic drink and should only be taken if prescribed by herbalists, when mixed with Sarsaparilla, for rheumatism and chronic skin complaints, although it is no longer used as an anti-syphilitic herb.

Sassafras oil, *which should not be used without medical advice*, can be helpful, used externally and very carefully, for relieving toothache.

It is possible to grow Sassafras trees in sheltered places in Britain. Their leaves are very attractive and assume good autumn colour, as well as having curious, non-uniform shapes. Young trees may be obtained from aboriculturists (such as Hilliers of Winchester, Hampshire).

**SAVORY, SUMMER\*** (*Satureja hortensis*). This is a garden herb which has been brought to cooler climates, by invaders, or travellers, possibly introduced, once again, by the Romans. It has a pleasant, Marjoram-like taste and is easy to cultivate.

It should be sown as seeds (although young plants can be obtained from some herb nurseries) and the seeds show great viability, for they will germinate even after being stored for some time. Summer Savory is an annual with pleasant aromatic virtues, and small mauve flowers. The flowers indicate when the herb should be cut, dried and stored for winter use as the plant is at its best when they are in full bloom.

A pleasing, refreshing carminative tisane can be made in the usual proportions from fresh or dried stems and leaves.

**SAVORY, WINTER** (*Satureja montana*). I find it difficult, as long as I keep my eyes shut, to tell the difference between the taste of these two herbs. I am told, however, that it is possible, even easy, as this Winter Savory has far the stronger taste.

This is a shrubby, evergreen *Satureja,* which grows on stony hillsides in mediterranean countries. It is not difficult to grow and is available for use all the year round. However, friends, with colder gardens than mine,

*Savory (winter)*

say that it is tender and needs protection from frost.

Winter Savory makes a useful addition to sauces, soups, stews and even as a paté-flavourer. It is useful too as a 'wind-dispelling' herb, when taken as a tisane — made with a teaspoonful of chopped leaves and young stems, infused in ½ pint (275ml) of boiling water.

**SCARLET PIMPERNEL** (*Anagallis arvensis*), Poor Man's Weatherglass. A lotion made in the usual way — 1 oz (25g) herb to 1 pint (575ml) of boiling water — makes a pleasant skin-wash and has the old country reputation of being a 'freckle-remover'. It is poisonous if taken internally.

**SCURVY-GRASS** (*Cochlearia officinalis*), Spoonwort, Scrooby-grass, Sailors' Friend. This wild plant usually grows near the sea, but it can also be seen along saline rivers and on mountains away from the coast. It is a renowned plant, historically, for it was found that when it was eaten by vitamin-deprived sailors, who had been on long voyages without fruit or vegetables, it quickly helped them to regain their health. As many of them were in a disgraceful and scrofulous state, it was no wonder that the plant was greeted with delight whenever it was found. Later on it was discovered that oranges, which were so much easier to carry on board ship, performed the same miraculous purpose.

It has been found, and herbalists still use this herb, that a tea made from 2 oz (50g) of the plant to 1 pint (575ml) of boiling water, is a useful and stimulating tonic, if taken in small doses of not more than a wineglassful at a time, before meals. It also improves the complexion.

The fact that the plant's Latin name describes it as an 'official' herb means that it and others similarly named were once included in the British Pharmacopoeia.

*Scurvy-grass*

*Senna*

**SENNA** (*Cassia angustifolia*). Everyone has heard of, or even been given Senna tea as a laxative. The strength of the infusion has always been governed by the number of dried pods, put into a vessel for the tea-making. It is worth understanding that Senna, used too strongly, can be a most harsh purgative and also that, if it is being taken by a woman who is suckling her child, its effect will be passed on through her milk.

Used carefully, *and not by nursing mothers,* Senna can be a helpful laxative which need not become habit-forming. It does not grow in Britain.

**SKULLCAP** (*Scutellaria laterifolia*), Mad-dog Scullcap. This species of Skullcap, which can also be spelt 'Scullcap', grows in America. It is used by herbalists to provide an excellent soothing and mind-calming herb, which is completely non-habit-

forming and harmless. Qualified herbalists frequently prescribe it as a bedtime, or even a day-time drink, when it is made into a tisane, Skullcap tablets can also be bought at health stores.

The plant also has tonic, astringent and general nervine qualities.

*Skullcap*

**SORREL\*** (*Rumex acetosa*), Green Sauce, Scabs, Cuckoo's Sorrow, Sour Suds. This herb grows in meadows and other grassy places and can be found in most parts of the British and European countryside. It is useful in salads, as a cooked vegetable and is an anti-scorbutic and vitamin-provider and can also be used as a mild diuretic.

Sorrel tea can be made, in the usual way, and is helpful for all the above purposes. It makes a good cooling drink for anyone with a fever, too but *beware of using Sorrel and any of its related species if dealing with acidly-inclined people, or anyone with forms of rheumatism* as it only tends to aggravate their condition. The best garden Sorrel is *Rumex scutatus.*

**SOUTHERNWOOD*** (*Artemisia abrotanum*), Old Man, Lad's Love, Moth-killer. This feathery-leaved and woody shrub is not found wild in Britain but is easy to cultivate here. It seems hardy enough in sheltered gardens and can be grown from cuttings and from young plants which are obtainable from many nurseries. It is strongly aromatic and delightful as a garden plant, with its grey-green appearance and it also has several household uses.

Southernwood can be gathered and dried as a 'sweet herb' and is said to keep away irritating pests, moths and fleas and can be used as an ingredient of *pot-pourri* and other fragrant herbal mixtures. It makes a refreshing herbal bath.

Taken in small doses, Southernwood tea is a stimulating, tonic drink. An infusion made slightly stronger than in the usual way for internal use, can be poured over the hair when it is being washed for a final and delightfully scented hair-rinse. It has always been said to be a good herb for the hair, and it is even claimed that it has the virtue of encouraging new hair to grow in balding areas. It is slightly disinfectant and was once used, in the same way as Lavender, to make into sachets to be carried in one's pocket during epidemics. These sachets of Southernwood were carried too, to be sniffed during long church services or meetings 'to prevent the owners thereof from sleeping at difficult times'.

*Strawberry (wild)*

**STRAWBERRY, WILD** (*Fragaria vesca*), Woodman's Delight. This wildflower comes up in young coppices and 'open' woodland in Britain, Europe and Northern Asia — indeed, everywhere except in the really hot countries. It is always a welcome sight

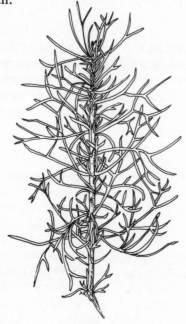

*Southernwood*

when the fruit is ripe, but the leaves too, when infusions are made in the usual way, and taken in small doses (not more than a wineglassful at a time), can also provide a helpful remedy for complaints needing laxative, diuretic and astringent help.

**SUNDEW** (*Drosera rotundifolia*), Flycatcher, Red Rot, Sticky-leaf. This uncommon wildflower grows only on acid, boggy soils where it is sometimes locally common and obvious from the shining red 'aura' of the hair-tips of its spoon-shaped leaves.

*It should never be used unless it is medically prescribed,* but when given by a doctor or a medical herbalist it can work wonders for bad, chronic coughs, especially whooping-cough. Plant biochemical research workers now find that it has antibiotic properties.

It has other virtues too, including that of being a tonic for the elderly. Used externally, the leaf-juice, being diluted carefully, is also believed to help in making curds and whey, and to

*Sundew*

be good for corns. Care must be taken, however, as this plant has not yet been fully investigated. It should be noted, also, that it is far too rare ever to be collected from any places where it is growing wild.

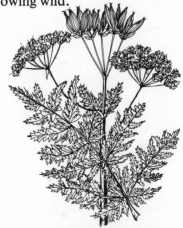

*Sweet Cicely*

**SWEET CICELY\*** (*Myrrhis odorata*), Sweets, Roman Plant, Sweet Fern, Wild Myrrh. This elegant plant, which is an early-flowering and beautiful member of the Umbelliferae, with its fern-like, white-blotched leaves and heads of white, scented flowers, grows wild only in Northern Britain and in Southern Europe. Actually, it is only a doubtful British native and may well have been introduced by monks and other travellers.

Sweet Cicely tea, made in the usual way, is a carminative, refreshing drink and a useful cough tonic. When the seed-pods are used alone, the result will be stronger and sweeter and reminiscent of the taste of aniseed.

A few leaves, or green seed-pods, act as a synergist if cooked with acid fruit like Gooseberries or Rhubarb and definitely make them taste sweeter, without having to use a lot of sugar. (See also explanation of the use of Angelica on page 38.)

**SWEET FLAG** (*Acorus calamus*), Sweet Sedge, Cinnamon Sedge, Floor-strewing Sedge. This flat-leaved, Iris-like plant is found by water, usually beside great lakes, or smaller 'stew-ponds', where it was once cultivated so that it could be cut, like hay, and used for strewing the floors of great halls, churches and monasteries. It is strongly aromatic, smelling always to me of oil of Citronella.

The leaves can easily be identified among those of Iris and sedges by their scent and because they are such a pale green. The flowers have to be searched for as they are all green and not particularly flower-like. They emerge from the inner edge of the upper third of the leaves, like green fingers and do not display any perianth segments.

*Sweet Flag*

Medically, it is the rhizomatous roots that are collected, dried and powdered down. Herbalists have used the powder from Sweet Flag roots for centuries as a stimulating tonic and an aromatic bitter. It was once used in Stockton Bitters, which was dispersed by chemists as a good appetite-increaser and for some types of 'giddy' headaches.

Tincture, or essence of *Calamus* can be obtained from herbal chemists only *after* it has been prescribed by a qualified herbalist for making an infusion or tea.

*Tansy*

**TANSY\*** (*Tanacetum vulgare*), Batchelors' Buttons, Stinking Willie, Traveller's Rest. Tansy is a wildflower growing by hedgerows, in damp river-side meadows, and on waste ground. It is a tall, handsome plant as its leaves are finely cut and fern-like and its flowering-heads form flat corymbs of round and very button-like golden, rayless 'daisies'.

Tansy usually comes out before Ragwort and when there are few other wild plants about of this gold colour, so it is obvious wherever it is growing. It can be grown in gardens, but it takes a lot of space.

It was used as a Passover herb, one of the bitter herbs that introduced the tonic element into the diet of people who had just ended their Lenten fast and a drink, made from the green herb was made on purpose 'to expel the worms that have grown lean with hunger'. This bitter drink was frequently given to children just for this purpose.

However, herbalists use this plant too, as a tonic and stimulant and, particularly, for girls and young women. Externally, Tansy lotion is a help when used as a hot poultice or fomentation, to soothe swollen joints.

Tansy tea should always be made very weak indeed, ½ oz (15g) of herb to 2 pints (about 1 litre) of boiling water is adequate. It should be sweetened before being taken, by the addition of a little honey.

**TARRAGON*** (*Artemisia dracunculus*), Little Dragon. This is a famous culinary herb and its aromatic leaves can be used in many ways. When grown in the garden, from young plants obtainable from herbal plant growers, the leaves and leafy branches can be cut in late summer and dried for winter use.

Actually the plant can be grown from cuttings, but it is a relatively tender herb and, in Britain and Northern Europe, it must be given winter

*Tarragon*

protection if there is any likelihood of frost. A covering of cut bracken fronds is often enough, unless the temperature is likely to drop very low.

Tarragon tea, made from a few leaves, 'makes a cordial drink which is a friend to the head, heart and liver'. Used as a mouthwash, Tarragon infusions have been used for generations to relieve toothache, and to help increase a poor appetite.

**TEA.**
See CAMELLIA.

**THYME, BASIL** (*Acinos arvensis*), Mountain Mint. Basil Thyme is a wild plant which grows on flinty chalk hillsides. Its country name may well be apt, but as I have only ever seen it growing on the Surrey and Sussex Downs, 'Mountain Mint' hardly applies, except that the naturalist, Gilbert White, referred to the Southdowns as 'mountains'.

Basil Thyme has larger and bluer flowers than the flowers of the ordinary wild or garden Thyme. It has been used for many purposes and Gerard, an early herbalist, said that 'it cureth them that are bittern of serpents; being burned or strewed, it drives serpents away; it taketh away black or blew spots that come by blows or beatings, making the skinne faire and white; but for such things, saith Galen, it is better to be laid to greene than dry'.

As an external lotion, an infusion of Basil Thyme is helpful for sciatica and neuralgia and it is also believed to make a calming skin-wash for those whose nerves are on edge.

This is one of the small, low growing plants that Southdown sheep used to keep so mat-like on the Downs because of their particular taste for it. Their preference for Basil Thyme was said to flavour their flesh and make it especially delicious. It is becoming a rare downland plant now that sheep have been replaced by heavier-footed cattle and now that rabbits, decimated by myxomatosis, no longer keep the turf short with their grazing.

*Thyme (Basil)*

**THYME\*** (*Thymus serpyllum* and *Thymus vulgaris*), Shepherd's Thyme, Mother Thyme. 'Mother', in herbal language often meant that the plant in question was used as a uterine remedy and Wild Thyme was probably used for several feminine purposes, including that of encouraging menstruation when periods were late. Nowadays, though, it is thought of as a flavourer of distinction, as a mild internal and external disinfectant and as a tea-making herb for those with chest complaints.

Thyme makes a soothing drink for the sleepless, too, especially when made in the usual way and then sweetened with honey and sipped while it is still hot. An infusion can be prepared by using 1 oz (25g) of fresh or dry herb to 1 pint (575ml) of boiling water.

All the cultivars of Thyme, including those with golden and with variegated leaves, are easy to grow from cuttings. Herbal nursery catalogues, as well as rock-garden specialists' lists, should be consulted for the different species, hybrids and cultivars which can give various flavours. Some of the Thymes are less procumbent than others but they are all inclined to get woody if they are not kept trimmed back at the end of every growing season. Their flowers are all much enjoyed by bees and the plants add much fragrance to all kinds of gardens, from window-boxes to large herbaceous border-edges.

**VALERIAN\*** (*Valeriana officinalis*), All-heal, Setwall, Capon's-tail. Valerian is a magnificent and ex-

*Valerian*

quisitely fragrant wild flower with a head of tiny, pale-pink flowers which are at their best around June/July, soon after midsummer. It grows in a wide variety of places, from dry downland slopes to damp meadows, varying in height according to the amount of moisture that is available to it. It should be sniffed at appreciatively when it is wild and left to go on growing, for it is easy to grow in gardens from seed or from young plants, if it is needed for making a soothing herbal tea.

Our wildflowers are now becoming too scarce, the places where they used to grow in profusion are quickly being given up for building or road-making purposes, for them to be gathered any longer. It is up to us all to look after them and conserve what there is left so that they can set seed and increase where they are, rather than being inter-fered with. So, apart from cultivated Valerian, the powdered root should be bought already prepared, from health shops or herbal chemists.

*Valerian, however, should not be used for making tisanes unless it is prescribed by a doctor or a medical herbalist.* It is a wonderfully soothing herb, promoting sleep, quieting exhausted nerves and acting as a strong sedative. It is also a painkiller. Probably, the careful use of this herb, in carefully worked-out doses, could save many troubles incurred by taking stronger sleep-inducing drugs.

The plant, like Catmint, is very attractive to cats and it is said that the Pied Piper of Hamelin attracted them and other animals in great numbers, by carrying it!

**VERVAIN** (*Verbena officinalis*), Herb of Grace, Holy Herb, Simpler's Joy, Devil's Hate, Wizard's Plant. These names show how much this little slender wildflower must have been venerated through the years. It is not even a particularly significant plant, although its minute lilac-coloured flowers can be eye-catching to botanists. It has the reputation of only growing within sight or actually within a mile of human habitation, but this does not always prove to be a reliable guide to finding it.

'Verbena' was a word generally used to denote a sacred herb, and also meant 'an altar herb'. Whether this plant's medicinal reputation has its origins in this belief or not is not fully understood yet. *It can be a dangerous herb for amateurs to use,* but in the hands of qualified medical practitioners, one dose can prove miraculous. It is used by homoeopaths and herbalists alike and the effect of an infusion, taken in a single dose, seems to have many beneficial results as a diuretic, or as a sleep-inducer and even 'to brighten up the patient's mental powers'.

**VIOLET, SWEET** (*Viola odorata*), Cuckoo's Shoe, Sweetling, Garland-flower. It seems profane, in some ways, to pick these enchanting, deliciously fragrant little flowers to use them for making a herbal drink. However, all country people do not think of them as beautiful, or even that they should be brought indoors at all; for Sweet Violets were once said to encourage fleas! But a few, discounting both points of view, can be picked and infused in a small vessel together with a teaspoonful of honey, just to see how they taste. Do not use many, for the stronger infusion may have laxative properties.

Violet leaves are now being carefully analysed and their medicinal virtues investigated. They certainly have

antiseptic properties and possibly act as antibiotics, and an infusion made in the usual way and taken in wineglassful doses is prescribed by herbalists for coughs and for those with difficult breathing. The infusion, if used as an external lotion, makes an excellent compress for various swellings and for the painful early stages of a developing sore throat.

Sweet Violets can, of course, be easily grown in gardens from seed and from young plants. Different forms of the plant, including, occasionally, the old-fashioned Parma Violets, are obtainable from specialist growers.

**VIPER'S BUGLOSS** (*Echium vulgare*), Blue Cats' Tail, Ironweed, Our Lord's Flannel, Blue Weed, Snakes' Flower. It would be impossible

*Viper's Bugloss*

*Violet (sweet)*

to overlook a field full of this tall, striking, wild, blue-flowered plant. The spires of first pink, then finally cobalt flowers are eagerly sought out by bees and some butterflies. It grows particularly well in chalky soils, but also in old gravel pits, on top of shingle beaches and in an assortment of other places.

Viper's Bugloss tea, made with the young leaves in the usual way, lifts headaches, relieves fevers, helps those with chest troubles and soothes tired nerves. It is also said to act as a cheering, cordial herb.

*Walnut*

**WALNUT\*** (*Juglans nigra*), Jupiter's Nuts. Walnut trees were probably introduced into Britain by the invading Romans, and are not particularly hardy. It does, however, take a really severely cold winter to kill off well-established trees completely.

Although most people enjoy the fruit, or nuts, and others use their green husks as dye-plants (with rubber gloves to stop the hands from being dyed as well), it is the leaves that are used to make a herbal infusion.

The old simplers gathered young leaves in early summer, when the 'morn was fresh and dry' and dried them off carefully for future use as an unbeatable complexion treatment. Actually, today's herbal practitioners still use Walnut lotion, made in the usual way, for an external application to help stubborn eczema, taking care to enquire into their patient's diet and changing it, so that the complaint is also helped inwardly, by vitamin-full but unspiced, bulk-providing and virtually sugarless meals.

**WATERCRESS** (*Nasturtium officinale*), Tongue-grass, Kerse, Tang-tongue, Carpenter's Chips. How sad it is that now, fresh Watercress can so seldom be picked from running streams with safety. Our land, air and water are so polluted that most of our water is completely unsafe for gathering edible plants, unless they have been carefully cultivated in filtered, shallow gravelled-bottomed beds.

*Watercress*

If you are fortunate enough to live near one of the accredited Watercress 'farms', make the most of it, for this herb provides all kinds of nutrients the body needs, including vitamins and trace elements of iron. A strong Watercress tisane, made with boiling water poured over a good handful of the green leaves and young juicy stems, makes a refreshing and appetite-restoring drink. Watercress, reduced to a green pulp in a juicer, can be used as a tonic and a complexion restorer. It can be added to home-made mayonnaise, or taken alone or even put in cold summer soups, with some salt. I use it as a starter, instead of fruit juice, before a big, rich meal.

**WATER VIOLET** (*Hottonia palustris*), Feather-foil, Cat's-eyes, Water Yarrow. This beautiful, but now rare, wildflower has been included in this

*Water Violet*

book because it is one of Dr Edward Bach's 'Twelve Healers'. If you have not yet read anything about this wonderful man who discovered a simple and natural way of using flowers for healing purposes, you can find out more from books issued by the Edward Bach Healing Centre (see *Useful Addresses*). He made his remedies sometimes by floating flowers in spring water and exposing them to the sun: a very rarified method of making a herbal infusion or herbal remedy.

**WHITLOW-GRASS** (*Erophila verna*), Wall-topper. This very small plant belongs to the same botanical family as the cresses, many of our cabbage-type vegetables and the wall-flowers. Its minute early-spring white flowers are so tiny that only few people spot it as it grows on gravelly paths and also on the top of walls. It is almost the earliest of all our wildflowers to appear.

Whitlow-grass has an ancient reputation as a 'herb for curing suppurating festers, especially those that appear near the finger-nails or toe-nails,' It is, in fact, excellent for making a lotion for a 'drawing' poultice, if you have the patience to gather, wash and infuse it. I tried a small handful to ½ pint (275ml) of boiling water, as the plant is plentiful in our village, and found it was very good.

**WITCH HAZEL\*** (*Hamamelis virginiana*), Winterbloom, Yellow Spider Plant. This is one of the herbal extracts

*Witch hazel*

which are still obtainable, in tincture and extract form, from most chemists. *It is strictly for external use* and when applied to the skin as a lotion, it helps bruises, sprains, and pulled muscles as well as sunburn, scalds, insect-bites and stings. When diluted and used in an eye-bath, Witch Hazel makes a useful 'refrigerating' astringent and a cooling, soothing lotion for hot and burning haemorrhoids.

**WOODRUFF, SWEET** (*Galium odoratum*), Wood-rove, Moth-herb. This sweet-smelling, somewhat insignificant wildflower loves growing under the trees in ash woods, early in the year before their full leaf-canopy makes the wood's floor dark. It used to be gathered as a strewing herb 'for my lady's chamber'. It was also used by herbalists to stimulate sick livers, or to relieve nausea. Nowadays it is not often prescribed, except by a few herbalists who use an infusion, taken by the wine-glassful three times daily, as a stomachic and tonic. In Germany, a flowering stem of Woodruff is floated in Rhine-wine-based hock; it is said to improve its flavour.

**WOOD SAGE** (*Teucrium scorodonia*), Gypsy's Baccy, Rock Mint, Wood Garlick Sage, Clear-beer. Wood Sage is an easy wildflower to recognize with its tough-stemmed, wrinkled-leaved upright spike, for it has only an unobtrusive spike of straw-coloured

*Woodruff (sweet)*

*Wood Sage*

flowers. As its last-named country name suggests, its leaves were put into home-made beer, while it was being made, to help clear it. It was also used to add a bitter and slightly spicy flavour. This herb is collected before it comes into flower in late summer and was widely used for making infusions for coughs and colds and for any internal inflammations. Now that medical herbalists and biochemists are working together to find out the more exact attributes of plants, it is only used, really, for a tonic herb, particularly one that will reduce a persistent slight, but regularly recurring temperature.

**WORMWOOD\*** (*Artemisia absinthium*), Mugwort, Old Woman. This is not really the *Artemisia* to which the name 'Mugwort' is usually applied (see page 85), Old Man, is of course, another *Artemisia* (see SOUTHERNWOOD), but Old Woman is a native of this country and certainly known in a rare but perhaps naturalized state growing near the coast. It is unmistakable because it is deliciously and strongly aromatic, which the truer Mugwort is not.

This plant also had a country name — Green Ginger — and has the reputation for being more bitter than any other known plant. It was used for a wide variety of purposes, including that of 'denying the snake its poyson', i.e. antidoting the venom in a snake's bite. It was also used to counteract the effect of eating poisonous toadstools.

Wormwood had to be gathered with

*Wormwood*

its flowers still fresh or just as it was about to produce seed. Thus, Thomas Tusser, in his *July's Husbandry* of 1571, wrote:

> Before Wormwood hath seed get a handful or twaine
> To save against March to make Flea to refraine.

It also was used in love-potions, but modern herbalists only use it as a tonic, particularly as a digestive and for flatulence. It is now also believed to stimulate the ductless glands, but should always be used with care, preferably only on professional recommendation.

Wormwood tea, made from 1 oz (25g) of the herb (fresh or dry) to 1 pint (575ml) of boiling water and allowed to stand and 'seethe' for 10-15 minutes, is helpful to 'frighten away the melancholy' or, in other words, to act as a cheering herb.

*Woundwort*

**WOUNDWORT** (*Stachys sylvatica*), Hedge Woundwort as opposed to Wood Woundwort, Betony, or Dusty Woundwort. This is one of the plants which grows in profusion along roadsides and also as a garden, wood and wasteland wildflower in many parts of Britain and Northern Europe. It has slightly downy leaves and late-summer spires of a muted beetroot-red, small flowers which are not obtrusive even though they may reach a height of two, or three feet tall. It is very popular with bumble-bees which probe into the little dull maroon lipped flowers for their nectar.

Hedge Woundwort has long been used to heal wounds, but modern herbalists do not seem very enthusiastic about its properties, although they do sometimes suggest infusing it as a tonic or cheering herb. *Amateurs should not try to make their own teas from it without a prescription and full instructions from qualified people.*

**YARROW** (*Achillea millefolium*), Milfoil, Bloodwort, Carpenters' Weed, Devil's Plaything, Angel-flower, Woundwort, Old Man's Pepper, Bunch o' Daisies, Hemming and Sewing, Staunchgrass, Staunch-weed. The great number of picturesque country names that can be found to describe this wildflower tell of its popularity and long use. It grows alongside lanes, roads, even motorways, and it is usually plentiful. Its 'Bunch o' Daisy' flower-heads are usually white, but they may be pink too.

Care should be taken, when picking any wild plants for medicinal or even for culinary use, not to take pieces of plants growing in any areas that may have been polluted by fumes from motor traffic.

*Yarrow*

Yarrow tea is still given by herbalists as a diaphoretic, or sweat-invoking, drink to reduce temperatures, particularly with Peppermint and Elder flowers for those with heavy colds or influenza. It should be made in the usual way — 1 oz (25g) of herb to 1 pint (575ml) of boiling water and drunk warm and sweetened, if preferred, with brown sugar or honey, in wineglassful doses. It can also be prescribed as a tonic and as a mild diuretic as well as for sufferers from cramp. Leaves for Yarrow tea should always be used fresh: flowers can be dried.

Externally, a lotion made in the same way makes a soothing application for sore piles, for toothache, as well as for bleeding wounds or scratches. If hurt far from home, crushed Yarrow leaves, rolled in the hand, as hard as possible, act as a temporary styptic to check the blood-flow.

Yarrow is another magic herb, 'assigned to St John' and is also a 'witch-discourager' which used to be used in the old days by country people to keep evil spirits away from their byres and stables, for the safety of their cattle and horses.

**ZEA TEA.**
See CORNSILK.

# PART THREE

# APPENDICES

# TABLE TO SHOW HERBS THAT CAN BE GROWN AT HOME

| NAME OF HERB | DESCRIPTION |
|---|---|
| ALFALFA (*Medicago sativa*) | Perennial green fodder herb with purple flowers. Needs cutting back yearly and using when young. Attracts bees. |
| ANGELICA (*Angelica archangelica*) | Large, space-taking, self-sowing perennial herb with wide heads of yellow/green flowers. Grows up to 79 ins (2m) tall. |
| ANISE (*Pimpinella anisum*) | Tender annual, needs frost-protection. Can grow to 20 ins (50cm). cm' |
| APPLE (*Malus domestica cultivars*) | Tree, giving pleasure at all seasons and providing fruit. Choice of cultivar and trained shape available from good tree-growing nurseries. Attracts bees. |
| BARLEY (*Hordeum* spp.) | Annual cereal grain-producing crop. Slender growth. |
| BASIL (*Ocimum basilicum*) | Tender annual herb, approximately 8-16 ins (20-40cm) tall. |
| BAY (*Laurus nobilis*) | Evergreen tree with aromatic leaves. Govern size and shape by careful pruning. |
| BERGAMOT (*Monarda didyma*) | Perennial with mop-heads of crimson or pink flowers. Needs dividing about every three years. Height 20-27 ins (50-70cm). |
| BIRCH (*Betula pendula*) | Native, deciduous tree. Can grow up to 50 ft (15m). |
| BISTORT (*Polygonum bistorta*) | Perennial herbaceous native plant. Height about 20 ins (50cm). |
| BLACKBERRY (*Rubus fructicosus*) | Scrambling thorny shrub needing annual pruning and tying. Choice of cultivar important. Good for bees and butterflies. |
| BLACKCURRANT (*Ribes nigrum*) | Shrub needing careful annual pruning, and plenty of space. |
| BLUE FLAG (*Iris versicolor*) | Decorative blue flower growing from tuberous roots, needing damp situation. |
| BORAGE (*Borago officinalis*) | Attractive annual herb with bright cobalt-blue flowers. Self-seeding in light soils. Bee-loved and sought. |
| BUTCHER'S BROOM (*Ruscus aculeatus*) | Spiny, evergreen, low shrub, useful ground-cover plant in shady situations. Needs dividing when thick. |
| CALAMINT (*Calamintha sylvatica*) | Perennial herbaceous plant. Height about 8-10 ins (20-25cm). |
| CARAWAY (*Carum carvi*) | Tender, often frail biennial herb, needing shelter. |
| CARROT (*Daucus carota*) | Root vegetable needing good light soil. |
| CATMINT (*Nepeta cataria*) | Attractive perennial flowering herb. Needs room for young flowering shoots to grow. Attracts bees and butterflies. |
| CELERY (*Apium graveolens*) | Garden vegetable needing care and good soil. Cultivar choice important as some are far easier to grow than others. |
| CHAMOMILE I (*Chamaemelum nobile*) | Usually annual, and often self-sowing. Can also over-winter to become perennial. Frail foliage, attractive white 'daisy' flowers. |
| CHAMOMILE II (*Matricaria recutita*) | Very similar to above. |
| CLEAVERS (*Galium aparine*) | Annual wayside hedge-scrambling weed; can be left to grow in wild places in garden. |
| COMFREY (*Symphytum officinale*) | Strong, coarse perennial herb, needing much room and good light. Sought out by bees. |

## WAYS IN WHICH TO PLANT

| Ways in which to plant | WHERE TO GROW | | | |
| --- | --- | --- | --- | --- |
| | Indoors | Window-box | Containers | Garden |
| From seed. | * | * | * | * |
| From stem, root-cuttings and root division. | | | * | * |
| From seed. | | | * | * |
| From young bought trees; can be tried from stem cuttings. | | | * | * |
| From seed. | * | * | * | * |
| From young bought plants or seed. | | * | * | * |
| Bought young trees, or stem cuttings. | | | * | * |
| From seed, root-cuttings and root division. | | | * | * |
| From seed or bought young tree. | | | | * |
| From seed, root-cuttings or division. | | | * | * |
| From bought plants. | | | * | * |
| From stem cuttings or bought plants. | | | * | * |
| From bought tuberous stock, subsequently by root division. | | | | * |
| From seed. | | * | * | * |
| From bought plants, then by root division. | | | | * |
| From seed, stem-cuttings and root division. | | * | * | * |
| From seed. | | * | * | * |
| From seed. | | | * | * |
| From root-cuttings and root division. | | | * | * |
| From seed. | | | | * |
| From seed. | | * | * | * |
| From seed. | | | * | * |
| From seed. | | | | * |
| From seed, root-cuttings and root division. | | | | * |

# TABLE TO SHOW HERBS THAT CAN BE GROWN AT HOME

| NAME OF HERB | DESCRIPTION |
|---|---|
| CORIANDER (*Coriandrum sativum*) | Frail annual herb, shy to produce seed, needs shelter. May reach 14-18 ins (30-45cm) tall. |
| CORNSILK or MAIZE (*Zea mays*) | Tall, space-taking annual grass which should not be planted out until frost is over. Height 39-79 ins (1-2m). |
| COSTMARY (*Chrysanthemum balsamita*) | Perennial herb which can grow to about 39 ins (1m). |
| CRESS (*Lepidium sativum*) | Annual herb needing little space as usually cut in first seedling growth. |
| CUMIN (*Cuminum cyminum*) | Rather frail annual herb needing sheltered situation. |
| DILL (*Anethum graveolens*) | Annual herb needing shelter. Grows up to 39 ins (1m) tall. |
| ELDER (*Sambucus nigra*) | Usually shrubby, native deciduous tree. Grows in poor soil. |
| ELECAMPANE (*Inula helenium*) | Tall, coarse perennial reaching almost 79 ins (2m) tall. |
| EVENING PRIMROSE (*Oenothera biennis*) | Biennial herb with flowering stem produced second season. Can reach 5 ft (1½m) tall. Attracts interesting moths. |
| FENNEL (*Foeniculum vulgare*) | Attractive, feathery-leaved perennial herb. Grows well from seed. Bronze-leaved type available. Tall. |
| FEVERFEW (*Chrysanthemum parthenium*) | Pale, but bright-green annual herb with heads of white 'daisy' flowers. Bushy form, can reach 1 ft (30cm). |
| FIG (*Ficus carica*) | Small deciduous tree. Needs careful root control and shelter. Choice of species bought important. |
| FLAX (*Linum usitatissimum*) | Annual fodder plant grown for seed (Linseed) or for stem fibres. Pretty blue flowers. Can reach 3 ft (90cm). |
| GARLIC (*Allium sativum*) | New cloves grow from bulbs planted annually. Has good antiseptic powers towards neighbouring plants. |
| GRAVEL-ROOT (*Eupatorium purpureum*) | Tall, coarse perennial — up to 79 ins (2m) — with good heads of dull purple flowers. Needs plenty of space. |
| GUELDER ROSE (*Viburnum opulus*) | Native shrub, more ornamental species and cultivars available from nurseries. Needs careful pruning to keep shape. |
| HAWTHORN (*Crataegus monogyna*) | Native tree, see above. |
| HOP (*Humulus lupulus*) | Twining perennial herb with decorative stems, leaves and flowering 'cones'. |
| HYSSOP — (*Hyssopus officinalis*) | Low perennial, forming shrub-like growth. Useful edging plant with bright blue flowers. Good for bees. |
| LAVENDER (*Lavendula angustifolia*) | As above, but with 'lavender' flowers. Can grow taller. Excellent for bees and butterflies. |
| LEMON BALM (*Melissa officinalis*) | Perennial, rampageous herb, needing control or will invade all beds. Flowers very bee-loved. |
| LEMON VERBENA (*Aloysia triphylla*) | Tender, deciduous shrub needing shelter, especially in winter, preferably against wall. Bee-loved. |
| LIME (*Tilia cordata*) | Uncommon wild tree in Britain. Can grow to 65-100 ft (20-30m). |

## WAYS IN WHICH TO PLANT

| Ways in which to plant | WHERE TO GROW | | | |
|---|---|---|---|---|
| | Indoors | Window-box | Containers | Garden |
| From seed. | | | | * |
| From seed. | | | * | * |
| From stem-cuttings or root-cuttings and root division. | | | * | * |
| From seed. | * | * | * | * |
| From seed. | | | * | * |
| From seed. | | | * | * |
| From seed, stem-cuttings or root division or young plants. | | | | * |
| From root-cuttings or root division. | | | | * |
| From seed. | | | | * |
| From seed, root-cuttings and young plants. | | | * | * |
| From seed. | | * | * | * |
| From stem-cuttings or layerings, or bought young tree. | | | | * |
| From seed. | | * | * | * |
| From bought bulbs, or cloves or offsets. | | * | * | * |
| From root division. | | | | * |
| From seed or stem-cuttings, or bought young plants. | | | | * |
| From seeds or stem-cuttings. | | | | * |
| From stem-cuttings or bought young plants. | | | * | * |
| From seed or root-cuttings. | | | * | * |
| From stem-cuttings. | | * | * | * |
| From seed or root-cuttings. | | | | * |
| From stem-cuttings or bought young plant. | | | * | * |
| From bought young tree. | | | | * |

# TABLE TO SHOW HERBS THAT CAN BE GROWN AT HOME

| NAME OF HERB | DESCRIPTION |
|---|---|
| LOVAGE (*Ligusticum scoticum*) | Wild, tall perennial; only found as a native plant growing on northern cliffs, but seed can be bought from herb-growers and it is easy to grow in gardens. |
| LUNGWORT (*Pulmonaria officinalis*) | Delightful, low, early-flowering perennial herb, decorative leaves and red and blue flowers. Attractive to bees. |
| MARIGOLD (*Calendula officinalis*) | Annual orange-flowered herb, grows up to 12-20 ins (30-50cm). Good for bees if single-flowered forms chosen. |
| MARJORAM (*Origanum onites*) | Exceptionally aromatic perennial herb. Good edging plant. Flowers very attractive to bees and butterflies. |
| MARSHMALLOW (*Althaea officinalis*) | Very handsome, grey-green-leaved, tall herbaceous plant. Perennial. |
| MINTS (*Mentha* spp.) | See Lemon Balm. Many different species and forms of Mint are available from tiny creeping *M. x requienii* to tall Apple Mint and Peppermint. |
| MULBERRY (*Morus nigra*) | Deciduous tree which can grow tall and wide, so place for planting must be chosen with care. |
| MUSTARD, WHITE (*Sinapsis alba*) | Annual cultivated herb grown to provide commercial crops of the condiment mustard. Height up to 1-2 ft (30-60cm). |
| PARSLEY (*Petroselinum crispum*) | Bright green, leafy annual or biennial herb of bushy habit. Makes good edging plant. Slightly tender. |
| PRIMROSE (*Primula vulgaris*) | Early-flowering, perennial, wild plant. Needs room for over-wintering leaf-rosette. |
| RASPBERRY (*Rubus idaeus*) | Fruiting shrub, needing careful annual pruning. Can reach 5 ft (1½m) tall. Good for bees. |
| ROSEMARY (*Rosmarinus officinalis*) | Evergreen, aromatic shrub with blue flowers nearly all year round. Slightly tender. Good for bees. |
| ROSE (*Rosa* spp. hybrids and cultivars) | Often a thorned shrub which can be of climbing habit. Decorative leaves with single or double white, yellow, pink or red flowers. A few species have variegated flowers. |
| ROWAN (*Sorbus aucuparia*) | Wild tree; grows up to 13 ft (4m) tall. Heads of orange berries (very attractive to birds), lovely in summer. |
| SAGE (*Salvia officinalis*) | Normally, grey-green-leaved shrub (can also be red, purple or variegated) with bright purple flowers. Can sprawl widely. Good for bees. |
| SAVORY, SUMMER (*Satureja hortensis*) | Annual needing shelter, only up to 12-16 ins 30-40cm) tall. |
| SAVORY, WINTER (*Satureja montana*) | Low evergreen perennial. Useful edging plant. |
| SORREL, FRENCH (*Rumex scutatus*) | Needs sowing annually from seed for best leaves. |
| SOUTHERNWOOD (*Artemisia abrotanum*) | Shrubby, feathery-leaved perennial. Height up to 39 ins (1m). |
| SWEET CICELY (*Myrrhis odorata*) | Perennial herb, with fern-like leaves. Height up to 39 ins (1m). Useful natural 'sweetener' for sour fruit. |
| TARRAGON (*Artemisia dracunculus*) | Slightly tender perennial. Can grow to 31 ins (80cm). |
| THYMES (*Thymus vulgaris, Thymus serpyllum,* hybrids and cultivars) | Low evergreen shrubs. Good for edging and bees. |

| WAYS IN WHICH TO PLANT | WHERE TO GROW: Indoors | Window-box | Containers | Garden |
|---|---|---|---|---|
| From seed or bought young plant. | | | * | * |
| From seed or root-cuttings. | | * | * | * |
| From seed. | | * | * | * |
| From stem-cuttings or root-cuttings or bought young plant. | | * | * | * |
| From bought plants; then root-cuttings. | | | | * |
| From root-cuttings or root division or bought young plants. | * | * | * | * |
| From bought young tree. | | | | * |
| From seed. | * | * | * | * |
| From seed. | * | * | * | * |
| From seed and root division. | | * | * | * |
| From stem-cuttings or bought plants. | | | * | * |
| From stem-cuttings or layering. | | | * | * |
| From stem-cuttings or bought species, cultivars and hybrids. | | | * | * |
| From seed or bought young tree. | | | | * |
| From stem cuttings. | | * | * | * |
| From seed. | | * | * | * |
| From stem-cuttings, root division or bought young plants. | | * | * | * |
| From seed. | | | * | * |
| From stem-cuttings. | | | * | * |
| From seed or root division. | | | | * |
| From seed or bought young plants. | | | * | * |
| From stem-cuttings, root division or layering. | | * | * | * |

# GLOSSARY

## Herbalists' Terms

*Alterative:* Herbs that help in restoring full healthy state of being.

*Anodyne:* Harmless substances that assuage pain.

*Antibiotic:* Substances which are able to injure or kill living bacteria.

*Antidote:* Remedies that help to counteract or relieve unpleasant effects caused by other substances.

*Aphrodisiac:* Sex stimulating herbs.

*Aromatic:* Herbs with spicy, fragrant and sweet scent from bark, leaf or flower.

*Astringent:* Substances which tighten, or help to contract the tissues.

*Cardiac:* Heart remedies.

*Carminative:* Herbs that are 'comforting' to the stomach and help to move, expel and lessen 'wind' and relieve nausea and other digestive troubles.

*Cathartic:* Remedies having a bowel-stimulating effect.

*Cordial:* Herbs that are invigorating to the heart.

*Decoctions:* Herbal preparations made by boiling parts of the plant for drinking purposes.

*Demulcent:* Herbs that are soothing.

*Diaphoretic:* Herbs that are sweat-provoking.

*Digestive:* Remedies that aid the digestion.

*Diuretic:* Herbs that increase the flow of urine.

*Emmenogogue:* Medicinal substance which helps to start the menstrual flow.

*Emollient:* A substance that is kind and soothing to the skin.

*Expectorant:* Remedies that help to expel phlegm from the bronchial tubes.

*Febrifuge:* Fever-reducing herbs and other medicines.

*Germicide:* In this case herbs which help to destroy germs.

*Infusion:* A liquid solution made by pouring boiling water onto herbs and letting them 'brew' for a specified time, or at least a few minutes.

*Invigorant:* Substances that are strength-stimulating.

*Laxative:* Remedies to help the

bowels to act.

*Mucilaginous:* Herbs that have 'gummy', glutinous effects.

*Nervine:* Remedies to quieten and soothe the nerves.

*Nutrients:* Any harmless provider of nourishment.

*Purgative:* Drastic laxatives.

*Restorative:* Remedies which help to restore strength, particularly after illness.

*Sedative:* In this case, herbs that soothe the nerves and bring about relaxation in a harmless tranquillizing way.

*Soporific:* Sleep-encouraging herbs.

*Stimulant:* Substances which help to raise functional activities of the body to faster reaction — but beware of over-use.

*Stomachic:* Invigorating tonic for stomach which help to increase the appetite.

*Styptic:* Substances used to halt surface-bleeding from slight skin damage.

*Tonic:* See 'Restorative'.

## Gardening Terms

*Annual:* A plant that grows from seed, then flowers and seeds and dies back, all in one year.

*Biennial:* A plant that takes two years to grow from seed and produces flowers and seeds in the second season.

*Deciduous:* Plants, usually shrubs and trees, which lose their leaves altogether in the autumn and grow new young ones in the following spring.

*Evergreen:* Plants that are leafy throughout the year, but which, of course, lose some leaves and grow new ones gradually to replace them.

*Perennial:* Plants that, once mature, go on producing new shoots and usually increasing as a 'colony' from year to year. Sometimes perennial means simply a plant which produces flowers every year.

*Shrub:* A perennial plant with tough woody stems of which there may be several, unlike the generally taller trees, which usually have only one woody trunk.

# USEFUL INFORMATION

**Herb Gardens**
Knowle, Sevenoaks, Kent.
Arley Hall, Northwich, Cheshire.
Midsomer Herb Garden, Midsomer
   Norton, Bath.
Gaulden Manor, Taunton, Somerset.
Hatfield Palace, Hertfordshire.
Dower House, Badminton, Avon.
Manor House, Cranbourne, Dorset.
Barnsley House, Cirencester,
   Gloucestershire.
Knightshayes House, Tiverton,
   Devonshire.
Hardwick Hall, Derbyshire.
The Old Rectory, Burghfield,
   Berkshire.
Cokes House, West Burton,
   Pulborough, Sussex.
Parham Park, Pulborough, Sussex.
Sissinghurst Castle, Kent.
Fulham Palace Gardens,
   London SW6
Greenwich Park, London.
Marndhill, Ardington, Berkshire.
Gravetye Manor, Nr East Grinstead,
   Sussex.
Royal Botanic Gardens,

Nr Richmond, Surrey.
Old House, Church Minshall,
   Cheshire.
Capel Manor Institute of
   Horticulture, Waltham Cross,
   Hertfordshire.
Hever Castle, Kent.
Manor House Herb Garden,
   Wadeford, Chard, Somerset.
Lorendon, Faversham, Kent.
Lullingstone Castle, Kent.
Scotney Castle, Kent.
Cambridge Botanic Garden,
   Cambridge.
Emmanuel College Garden,
   Cambridge.
Edinburgh Botanic Garden,
   Edinburgh.
Womens' Institute Education Centre,
   Denham, Buckinghamshire.
Stone Cottage, Hambleton,
   Leicestershire.
South Collingham House,
   Collingham, Nottinghamshire.
Bampton Manor, Bampton Troy,
   Ewelme, Oxfordshire.
Gaulden Manor, Totland,

Shropshire.

Acorn Bank, Temple Sowerby,
 Nr Penrith.

Hidcote Manor, Chipping Campden,
 Gloucestershire.

Chelse Physic Garden, London SW3
 (by special permit only).

Anne Hathaway's Cottage,
 Stratford-on-Avon, Warwickshire.

Hollywell House, Swanmore,
 Hampshire.

Castle Drogo, Devonshire.

Moseley Old Hall, Staffordshire.

Westbury Court, Gloucestershire.

Felbrigg Hall, Lincolnshire.

The Mill House, Lower Ufford,
 Suffolk.

Priorwood Gardens, Melrose,
 Scotland.

The Bible Garden, Bangor, Wales.

St Fagan's Garden, Cardiff, Wales.

Springhill, Co. Londonderry, Ireland.

## Scented Gardens for the Blind

In public parks in Bournemouth,
Canterbury, Hove, Walthamstow
(London). Queen's Park, Harbourne,
Birmingham and Canbury Gardens,
Kingston-on-Thames, Surrey.

*(N.B. Remember always to send
adequately sized s.a.e. for replies.)*

## Herb Growers

Mrs Mary Alexander, Green Farm
 Cottage, Thorpe Green, Thorpe
 Morieux, Bury St Edmunds,
 Suffolk (Mint specialist).

Ashfields Herb Nursery, Hinstock,

Market Drayton, Shropshire.

Dorwest Herb Growers, Shipton
 Gorge, Bridport, Dorset.
 (Postal service *only*.)

Heches Herbs, St Peter in the Wood,
 Channel Islands.

The Herb Centre, Thornby Hall,
 Thornby, Northampton.

The Herb Farm, Southwaite,
 Carlisle.

The Herb Garden, Thunderbridge,
 Nr Huddersfield, Yorkshire.

Herbs from the Hoo, 46 Church St,
 Bucken, Huntingdon,
 Cambridgeshire.

Hullbrook House Herb Farm,
 Shamley Green, Guildford, Surrey.

The Old Rectory Herb Garden,
 Ightham, Kent.

Suffolk Herbs, Sawyer's Farm,
 Little Conard, Sudbury, Suffolk.

Sutton Manor Herb Farm, Sutton
 Scotney, Winchester, Hampshire.

Mrs J. Tippell, 57 Ormesby Way,
 Kenton, Harrow, Middlesex.

Tresare Herb Farm, Taman Bay,
 Looe, Cornwall.

## Herb Seeds

Chase Compost Seeds Ltd, Benhall,
 Saxmundham, Suffolk.

Dobie's Seeds, Upper Dee Mills,
 Llangollen, Clwyd, Wales.

Down to Earth Seeds, Cade
 Horticultural Products,
 Heathfield, Sussex.

The Seed Bank, 44 Albion Road,
 Sutton, Surrey.

Thompson and Morgan, Seedsmen,
 London Road, Ipswich, Suffolk.

**Frozen Herbs** (Wholesale only)
Hereford Herbs, Ocle Pychard,
　　Hereford.

**Bee Breeders**
Ilex Farm, Clay Cross, Handley,
　　Chesterfield.

*Bees:* It always seems that bees,
bumble-bees and herb gardens ought
to go together and that a herb garden or
a very floriferous garden of any kind,
provided no poisonous pesticides or
herbicides are used at all, provides an
excellent base for a hive or two of honey
bees. The flowers themselves will
attract the valuable bumble-bees which
make their own nests, often in the
earth.

　　It is very important, however, that
any intending bee-keeper should
realize that hived colonies of honey or
hive bees, need regular care and
attention, so that the responsibility of
keeping them must be fully understood, before any new honey-making
projects are undertaken.

　　Members of local branches of The
Beekeepers' Association (addresses
often to be found through telephone
directories or public libraries) will
usually offer helpful advice.

**Suppliers of Dried Herbs**
Baldwins, 173 Walworth Road,
　　London SE17
Colne Valley Foods Ltd, 714 London
　　Road, Leigh-on-Sea, Essex.
Culpeper's Shops: various branches

in London and Provinces (see
　　telephone directories).
D. Napier & Sons Ltd, 17/18 Bristol
　　Place, Edinburgh.
Potters (Herbal Supplies) Ltd,
　　Leyland Mill Lane, Wigan,
　　Lancashire. (Through Health
　　Stores and Herbal Shops and their
　　retail outlets.)
Nature's Way, Hall Lane, Haigh,
　　Wigan, Lancashire (Mail Order
　　Service).

**Supplier of Plant Tinctures**
John Eiles M.P.S., The Galen
　　Pharmacy, 1 South Terrace,
　　South St, Dorchester, Dorset.

**Miscellaneous Addresses**
National Institute of Medicinal
　　Herbalists Ltd. List of members
　　from the Registrar, School of
　　Herbal Medicine, 148 Forest
　　Road, Tunbridge Wells, Kent.
Edward Bach Foundation Centre,
　　Mount Vernon, Sotwell,
　　Wallingford, Oxfordshire.
The Herb Society, 34 Boscobel Place,
　　London SW1.
Henry Doubleday Research
　　Association (for all problems about
　　organic gardening and harmless
　　pest control), Bocking,
　　Braintree, Essex.
Aromatic Oil Co., 12 Littlegate St,
　　Oxford.
The Downland Craft Centre (Agents
　　for special herbal tea-pots),
　　Amberley, Arundel, West Sussex.
　　(Details on request.)

# THERAPEUTIC INDEX

**Abrasions,** Barley
**Abscesses,** Fenugreek, Figwort, Marshmallow
**Acidity,** Coriander, Meadowsweet
**Adrenal glands,** Borage
**Alterative,** Betony, Blackberry, Celandine (Greater), Couch Grass, Hops, Pipsissewa, Sarsaparilla
**Antibacterial,** Elecampane
**Antibiotic,** Agrimony, Cress, Sundew
**Antidote, to poison,** Wormwood
**Anti-scorbutic,** Bilberry, Cress
**Antiseptic,** Avens, Basil, Bearberry, Cress, Garlic, Marigold, St John's Wort, Violet
**Aphrodisiac,** Rosemary with Hibiscus
**Appetite, increasing,** Dandelion, Fennel, Fenugreek, Ginseng, Hops, Mustard, Myrrh, Tarragon
**Arthritis,** Coriander
**Asthma,** Butcher's Broom, Evening Primrose, Garlic
**Astringent,** Avens, Bearberry, Betony, Bistort, Blackberry, Camellia, Gravel Root, Knotgrass, Myrrh, Plantain, Raspberry, St John's Wort, Skullcap, Strawberry (Wild)

**Babies, illness in,** Chamomile, Dill
**Bath additive,** Chamomile
**Biliousness,** Celandine (Greater), Parsley Piert, Woodruff (Sweet)
**Bladder troubles,** Bearberry, Buchu, Parsley Piert
**Blood purifier,** Agrimony, Blue Flag, Burdock, Centaury, Heather Sassfras
**Boils,** Chickweed, Fenugreek, Marshmallow
**Bones, mending,** Comfrey
**Bowel complaints,** Bilberry, Bistort
**Bronchitis,** Butcher's Broom, Elecampane, Mustard (White)
**Bruise,** Arnica, Calamint, Hops, Witch Hazel
**Burns,** Comfrey, Marigold, Nettle

**Carbuncles,** Chickweed, Marshmallow
**Carminative,** Angelica, Bay, Caraway, Catmint, Chamomile, Cinnamon, Coriander, Cumin, Dill, Fennel, Ginger, Juniper, Lemon Balm, Marjoram, Rosemary, Sage, Savory (Summer), Sweet Cicely
**Catarrh,** Buchu, Hyssop
**Cheering herbs,** Borage, Lily-of-the-Valley, Meadowsweet, Sage, Wormwood, Woundwort
**Chest troubles,** Hyssop, Thyme, Viper's Bugloss
**Chilblains,** Arnica
**Colds,** Calamint, Cinnamon, Liquorice, Wood Sage, Yarrow

**Complexion improver,** Blue Flag, Chamomile, Chickweed, Couch Grass, Cucumber, Fumitory, Ground Elder, Heather, Lime, Marshmallow, Mint, Scurvy Grass, Walnut, Watercress
**Cooling herbs,** Burdock
**Cordials,** Blackcurrant, Borage, Calamint, Hawthorn, Rosemary, Tarragon, Viper's Bugloss
**Corns,** Sundew
**Coughs,** Anise (Aniseed), Comfrey, Elecampane, Flax, Liquorice, Lungwort, Mustard, Sundew, Sweet Cicely, Wood Sage
**Cramp,** Guelder-Rose, Mullein
**Cystitis,** Bearberry, Buchu, Cornsilk, Pipsissewa

**Demulcent,** Chickweed, Cornsilk, Fenugreek, Liquorice, Marshmallow, Parsley Piert, Pellitory-of-the-Wall, Rice
**Diabetes,** Bilberry
**Diaphoretic,** Calamint, Elder, Gravel-Root, Hawkweed (Mouse-Eared), Hyssop, Lemon Balm, Sage, Sarsaparilla, Sassafras, Yarrow
**Diarrhoea,** Avens, Bilberry, Comfrey, Knotgrass, Plantain, Rowan
**Digestive,** Angelica, Anise (Aniseed), Carrot, Lime, Quassia, Rhooibosch, Wormwood
**Disinfectant,** Cinnamon, St John's Wort, Southernwood, Thyme
**Diuretic,** Barley, Bladderwrack, Burdock, Celery, Cleavers, Cornsilk, Dandelion, Gravel-Root, Juniper, Parsley Piert, Pipsissewa, Sorrel, Strawberry (Wild), Yarrow
**Dropsy,** Butcher's Broom
**Dysentry,** Avens
**Dyspepsia,** Ginseng

**Eczema,** Celandine (Greater), Figwort, Walnut
**Emollient,** Blue Flag, Liquorice, Marshmallow
**Epilepsy,** Garlic
**Expectorant,** Angelica, Anise (Aniseed), Calamint, Hyssop, Lemon Verbena, St John's Wort
**Eye bath,** Witch Hazel
**Eye inflammation,** Eyebright

**Fatigue,** Lavender, Lime
**Febrifuge,** Centaury, Elder
**Fertilizer,** Fenugreek
**Fever,** Apple, Centuary, Elder, Lemon, Marjoram, Sorrel
**Flatulence,** Wormwood
**Foot bath,** Arnica, Sage
**Freckles,** Cleavers, Heather, Scarlet Pimpernel

**Garden pesticide,** Elder
**Gargle,** Avens, Blackberry, Lovage, Rowan, Sage
**Gout,** Birch (Silver), Butcher's Broom, Mullein

**Hair lotion,** Arnica, Chamomile, Lime, Marjoram, Mint, Rosemary, Sage, Southernwood
**Hands, softener,** Blue Flag, Cucumber
**Hangover,** Hops, Sassafras
**Headaches,** Bergamot, Betony, Feverfew, Lime, Sage, Viper's Bugloss
**Hysteria,** Betony, Chamomile, Moccasin Flower (Yellow)

**Indigestion,** Chamomile, Mint
**Inflammations, internal,** Wood Sage
**Influenza,** Yarrow
**Insect bites/stings,** Marigold, Nettle, Plantain, Sage, Witch Hazel
**Insect repellants,** Avens, Marjoram, Mint, Mugwort, Southernwood
**Invigorant,** Lavender

**Jaundice,** Butcher's Broom, Celandine (Greater)
**Joints, aching,** Ground Elder
**Joints, swollen,** Hops, Tansy

**Kidney complaints,** Marshmallow, Pellitory-of-the-Wall

**Laxative,** Dandelion, Feverfew, Fig, Fumitory, Mulberry, Prunes, Rhubarb, Senna, Strawberry (Wild), Violet
**Lungs, inflammation,** Comfrey

**Migraine,** Feverfew
**Mouthwash,** Blackberry, Mint, Myrrh
**Muscular injuries,** Arnica, Witch Hazel

**Nail-biting, deterrent,** Quassia
**Nausea,** Basil, Bergamot, Cinnamon, Mugwort, Woodruff (Sweet)
**Nervine,** Camellia, Guelder-Rose, Knotgrass, Rosemary with Hibiscus, St John's Wort, Skullcap, Viper's Bugloss
**Neuralgia,** Hedge Garlic, Mullein, Basil Thyme
**Nose bleeding,** Bistort, Hawkweed (Mouse-Eared), Knapweed (Greater)

**Pain killer, external,** Arnica, Chervil, Comfrey, Marigold
**Pain killer, internal,** Valerian
**Piles,** Bistort, Celandine (Lesser), Comfrey, Hawkweed (Mouse-Eared), Plantain, Witch Hazel, Yarrow
**Pregnancy,** Raspberry

**Quinsy,** Cudweed

**Rheumatism,** Alder, Birch (Silver), Bladderwrack, Borage, Celery, Coriander, Hedge Garlic, Nettle, Sassafras

**Scalds,** Comfrey, Marigold, Nettle, Witch Hazel
**Sciatica,** Basil Thyme
**Sedative,** Celery, Hops, Lettuce (Wild), Oats (Wild), Orange Buds, Primrose, Valerian
**Skin complaints,** Celandine (Greater), Figwort, Nettle, Sassafras
**Skin-wash,** Elder, Ground Elder, Pellitory-of-the-Wall, Plantain, Rosemary, Scarlet Pimpernel, Basil Thyme
**Sleeplessness, aid to,** Chamomile, Cleavers, Couch Grass, Lettuce (Wild), Lime Mate, Mint, Moccasin Flower (Yellow), Oats (Wild), Thyme, Valerian, Vervain
**Slimming,** Bladderwrack, Celery, Chickweed, Cleavers, Dandelion, Mate
**Smoking, discouraging,** Plantain
**Sores,** Burdock, Flax, Whitlow-Grass
**Sprains,** Arnica, Figwort, Marjoram, Witch Hazel
**Stimulant,** Alfalfa, Angelica, Borage, Camellia, Catmint, Cinnamon, Fennel, Lovage, Sassafras, Scurvy-Grass, Sweet Flag, Tansy
**Stomachics,** Caraway, Costmary, Hyssop, Lemon, Rosemary with Hibiscus, Woodruff (Sweet)
**Styptic,** Bistort, Knotgrass, Marigold, Plantain, Yarrow
**Sunburn,** Comfrey, Fumitory, Nettle, Plantain
**Swellings,** Alder, Figwort, Violet
**Synergic,** Angelica

**Temperature, reducing,** Yarrow
**Throat, sore,** Pellitory-of-the-Wall, Violet
**Tonic herbs,** Agrimony, Angelica, Betony, Birch (Silver), Blackberry, Blue Flag, Borage, Burdock, Calamint, Catmint, Centaury, Elder, Ginseng, Hawthorn, Hops, Hyssop, Lily-of-the-Valley, Marjoram, Mate, Mugwort, Myrrh, Pipsissewa, Primrose, Quassia, Rhooibosch, Sage, St John's Wort, Skullcap, Southernwood, Sundew, Watercress, Wood Sage, Wormwood, Woundwort, Yarrow
**Toothache,** Marjoram, Mullein, Plantain, Sassafras, Tarragon, Yarrow

**Ulcers, external,** Burdock, Goosefoot, Marigold, Sarsaparilla
**Ulcers of the mouth,** Cudweed
**Ulvers, of the stomach,** Comfrey, Liquorice
**Urinary troubles,** Bearberry, Bilberry, Borage, Cleavers, Cornsilk, Couch Grass, Flax, Gravel Root, Parsley, Parsley Piert

**Vermifuge,** Garlic, Hyssop
**Veterinary herbs,** Elecampane, Flax, Garlic

**Warts,** Celandine (Greater)
**Weight, increase,** Alfalfa
**Whopping cough,** Hawkweed (Mouse-Eared)
**Wind, dispelling,** Angelica, Cumin, Dill, Lovage, Mint, Savory (Winter)
**Worms,** Tansy
**Wounds,** Comfrey, Cress, Goosefoot, Marigold, Plantain, St John's Wort, Yarrow